The Unspoken:
A Glimpse Of Gang And Street Culture In Barbados

by

Kim L. Ramsay

© 2023 by Kim L Ramsay

First published 2023.

All rights reserved.

The use of any part of this publication, reproduced, transmitted in any form or by any means, electronic, mechanical, photocopying, recording, or otherwise, or stored in a retrieval system, without the prior written consent of the publisher is an infringement of the copyright law.

Ramsay, Kim L.

The Unspoken:
A Glimpse Of Gang And Street Culture In Barbados

ISBN 9798388137159

Printed and bound by COT Holdings Limited,
Barbados, West Indies

Contents

Acknowledgements vii

Disclaimer viii

A Word From The Author ix

About the Author x

Introduction xi

CHAPTER ONE
Warring Factions 1

CHAPTER TWO
The Pine 5

CHAPTER THREE
Historical Context Of The Gang Situation 13

CHAPTER FOUR
The Culture Of The Street 19

CHAPTER FIVE
Defining Gangs 25

CHAPTER SIX
From Gang Life To Christ 35

CHAPTER SEVEN
The Life Of Ken – A Dormant Gun Man 45

CHAPTER EIGHT
Kool And The Gang 53

CHAPTER NINE
The CNN Gang 57

CHAPTER TEN
Jesus And The Disciples 73

Contents

CHAPTER ELEVEN
Scare Dem Crew/ Bird Gang 81

CHAPTER TWELVE
Bloods And Crips 87

CHAPTER THIRTEEN
Chapman Lane And The Orleans 103

CHAPTER FOURTEEN
Community Urchin To Community 'Boss' 113

CHAPTER FIFTEEN
Janet: How Incest Scarred Her Life 119

CHAPTER SIXTEEN
"How Drug Addiction Almost Killed Me" 127

CHAPTER SEVENTEEN
The Role Of Women In Street Culture 133

CHAPTER EIGHTEEN
Evolution Of The Streets And Gang Culture 137

CHAPTER NINETEEN
Social Exclusion And The Street Culture 151

CHAPTER TWENTY
Discussion 157

CHAPTER TWENTY ONE
Solutions 163

ADDENDUM
Is History Repeating Itself? 167

Acknowledgements

I wish to thank the following for their contribution to this book:

My editors Leslie Lett Jr and David Straughn; Kathie Daniel of Southpaw Grafix for the cover; Mel Yearwood for the layout of the book; Andrew Searles, Attorney-at-law; Karen Ramsay; Monie Barrow of the Nation Library; Yvonne Norville of the Barbados Advocate Library; all persons who facilitated interviews including the gatekeepers; former and current members of gangs; persons in the wider community who are a part of the street culture; former Member of Parliament, Hamilton Lashley and other community activists, members of communities mentioned in this book; the Acting Superintendent of Prisons, DeCarlo Payne; Chief Officer Mark Corbin; Head of the Female Prison, Mrs. Sophie Drakes, inmates and all other persons not mentioned but who contributed quietly.

Disclaimer

While some **names and locations have been slightly altered** in many of the cases, everything else remains authentic in these accounts from former and current gang members.

The stories recounted are true and represent the actual facts surrounding the life on the streets.

Reader discretion is advised. The material, facts and language of these accounts are graphic and abrasive; and may be offensive to some.

A Word From The Author

This book is a historical account of gangs, street culture and some of the unspoken in Barbados. It has dissected these groupings to the level of individuals; and now speaks to their lives, their experiences, victimization, the crimes they committed, and gives a glaring view into the dark internal functioning of a parallel society.

As a researcher on crime, I understand that the topic of gangs can be sensitive. Many persons have died or been seriously injured at the hands of gang men. Some of their actions have terrorized communities and wider society. Many of these men were violent and engaged in terrifying acts.

However, it is important to capture history, even if this history is distasteful and dark. One aspect of research is oral histories, which gives the readers a snapshot of the past (and present) from those who have lived and experienced it, in their own words.

Understanding the streets and the social interactions, processes and structure of this underbelly of society offers readers a comprehensive analysis of the problem of criminality. Many of these men and women interviewed have similar backgrounds – poverty, expulsion from school, trauma (both physical and emotional), social exclusion and environmental influences that have shaped who they are.

Therefore, this book is not to glorify, but to give a fuller picture of the issues that have emerged. It allows for a broader perspective of the streets placing Street Culture into its true context that many would not have understood.

About the Author

Kim L Ramsay

Kim Ramsay is a criminologist with over 20 years experience, trained at the University of Leicester in the United Kingdom.

She is a Senior Researcher with the Government of Barbados and has conducted research on issues related to crime and the criminal justice system. Her main research interests are penal policy, criminal justice reform and research on violence and violence prevention.

She has carried out research on homicides; gangs and recidivism of ex-prisoners. She has also conducted a public opinion survey on crime; juvenile delinquency and fear of crime.

Kim is a part time lecturer in Criminology at The University of the West Indies where she has been teaching for close to 20 years.

Kim Ramsay is the author of four other books: **Barbados' Most Wanted, Murders that Shocked Barbados, The Barbados Prison System: Chronicles of Incarceration, Death, Riots and Reformation** and **Sex, Drugs & Murder – Unsolved Murders In Barbados**.

Introduction

In all societies lies an underworld and a subculture commonly referred to as "The Streets," which operate parallel to the mainstream society. This sub-culture is one in which the drug trade, gun smuggling, shootings, organized crime and corruption at all levels of society thrive. Alienation and social exclusion brought about by poverty and lack of skills exist. Street culture is one in which behaviours typically frowned upon in the mainstream, are respected, emulated, and sought after by the young and impressionable; primarily males. Most importantly, the streets operate with a strict code... a code of silence to authorities, a code where the **'system'** is *The Enemy* and anything representing the 'system' is to be despised and rejected. Here, an anti-authority belief structure is established, adopted and expected on the streets; it is handed down from generation to generation like a shining badge of honour. This belief structure is reflected in the attitudes and behaviours of those who live '*The Streets*'.

Ironically enough, the subculture of the streets and mainstream society covet the same things – wealth, privilege and a comfortable way of life. Many times, members of the subculture and mainstream society forge alliances - sometimes symbiotic; sometimes cynical and exploitative, often uneasy, always strategic; in pursuit of realizing these ultimate goals.

Jonathan Ilan in his book *Understanding Street Culture* (2015) refers to this culture as an "embodiment of frustration and discontent, fleeting emotional satisfactions and refusal to obey normative imperatives." (pg 152).

Street culture engages in a stipulated set of informal rules and behaviours which is accepted as the norm and which govern social interaction with most people (Anderson, 1999). Anderson also states that the street culture infers physicality and ruthlessness where manhood and respect go hand in hand. It should be noted here that 'Respect' is a profoundly significant concept in the culture of the street. This would go a long way in explaining the warring between two men or groups of men. Research indicates that these men are usually involved in disputes – one off and/or ongoing - over simple matters which tend to escalate, oftentimes with catastrophic consequences. The comparatively easy access and availability of firearms in Barbados only exacerbates the problem.

Gang activity, which encompasses all the following (the drug trade, gun smuggling, shootings, organized crime and corruption) is also part of the street culture.

Gangs have existed in Barbados for decades and have evolved over time. Gangs and street culture are notoriously difficult to access for research purposes (Sanders et al 2010). Even though the literature states that difficulties experienced in conducting gang research can be overcome by interviewing community members aligned with the gangs, this too proves difficult. Understandably, there is a great deal of fear about divulging too much information about the streets among those who live and work closely with them.

This book delves into this Street Culture and examines some of the gangs which existed from the 1970's and which currently exist in Barbados. The emerging issues mentioned above will be discussed. Some of the stories may shock the reader; some may intrigue and some may even disturb. This is the nature of the work of crime researchers.

I believe it is crucial to highlight for the reader what is, for the most part, *UNSPOKEN*; to educate and inform about the underbelly of society, about the past street culture and to briefly discuss its evolution and most importantly, to foreground the lessons which can be, and indeed, **should** be learned from these stories.

This book also attempts to give a more in-depth and personalized view into the evolution of gangs, the structure, ethos and modus operandi of these gangs and groups. Some of the most notorious members of these organisations will be highlighted, as well as the circumstances leading to conflicts between and among these gangs.

The author met privately with current and retired leaders and also with members of some of these gangs, to gather firsthand information and anecdotes about their lives in the gang and their motives and reasons for entering and exiting gang life. Most importantly, the author tried to ascertain how they perceived the grouping – whether as a gang or a brotherhood and where (if at all) these lines became blurred.

The book will end with best practices in community-based youth violence prevention with the roles of state and non-state actors.

CHAPTER ONE

Warring Factions

Warring communities

From time immemorial, groups and communities have been in conflict with each other. Some communities have been at war for decades and have continued in this vein for generations. This is not a problem unique to Barbados. In Jamaica for example, Tivoli Gardens and Denham Town have been warring for generations.

Some wars have been ignited over drugs, the supply and/or access to end users (the market or turf is seen as their own); and then the conflict spirals out of control. In many cases, what men/gangs were originally fighting about becomes lost in the war. In other cases, generations of men were, and still are warring without even knowing why; the reason lost with the passage of years. "They just know that you and another community do not get along and you are not supposed to venture into that community," explained one man from the street.

"Wars started when men started to lime. Men started to lime in their space and eventually created a name for themselves. They started doing illegal activities together and it evolved. The space created a leader, a man who has connections and can make things happen and it developed," said a member of the community.

Men who limed and congregated in one community started to war with men who limed and congregated in other areas of that same community or other communities over things that made little sense.

For example, many years ago there were ongoing conflicts between groupings like Dungeon and Academics, who were both from the Pine. They would war constantly. However, elders in the community brought the men together and that particular war was eventually resolved and settled. (Please see Chapter 2 on the Pine).

As one community activist opined, "It is a rat race, where there are no winners. Who isn't getting killed, is going to prison."

Both philosophical and anecdotal explanations have been offered on this issue of warring communities.

Community violence has been described as violence between people who are unrelated, and who may or may not know each other, usually outside the home. It is a widespread problem that affects all of us, particularly people who are disproportionately impacted by poverty, racism, and/or a lack of educational and economic opportunities. Assaults, shootings in public areas like schools and communities, fights among gangs and other groups ... all of these are examples of community violence.

The root causes of this community violence are established over generations. Research also suggests that certain characteristics of neighbourhoods can prevent or provoke violence.

The Urban Peace Institute has identified 10 factors that lead to community violence. These are outlined in Figure 01.

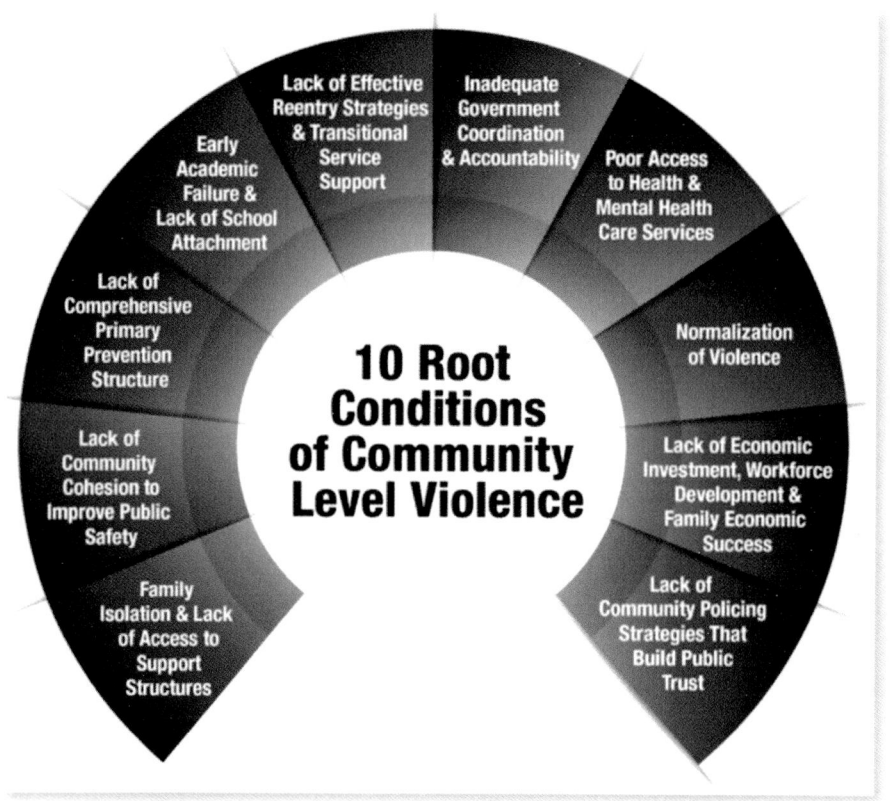

Figure 01: 10 Root Conditions of Community Level Violence

Warring groups

Many wars between communities usually start when simple, resolvable disagreements between individuals or groups are allowed to escalate. These group wars are not new and have been going on for decades.

Explanations have been offered for these wars, which have caused many deaths and injuries over time. Drugs, women, guns, turf, and petty arguments, have all been advanced as being triggers for the violence. Even looking at someone "the wrong way" could start a war between individuals and which could expand into groups and then engulf entire communities.

"If it [an incident] happened in the Orleans for instance, one man would go across and deal with a Chapman Lane man, and get into a scene, his posse would defend him so the war will increase," said a person who limes in the Orleans area.

One person said that many of these men who fight with each other actually went to school together or were raised among each other. As they got older, some of them would even pick up old generational wars as well.

For instance, in April 1993, police were called in about 8:00 pm to Hindsbury Road after some men had opened fire on a group of people gathered in the area. Five men on bicycles had ridden up to the group. They asked for a specific person, and on receiving no response, they pulled out guns – one a pipe gun and the other a shotgun – and opened fire with three shots into the crowd, injuring two men with pellets. One man, Ian, was shot in his buttocks and had to be rushed to the Queen Elizabeth Hospital.

Just hours later, an armed group went to a family's home at Richmond Gap, St Michael and fired a shot at a man in a verandah where other people, including children who were playing, were present.

There were also wars between blocks such as the Gulf Massive and the Persian Gulf from two neighbouring St Michael districts of Whitehall and Storey Gap respectively. According to the Report on Unattached Youth, (pg 4), a block has been described as "more than just a physical space in the community, where boys lime and hang out. Differentiated from other meeting places, the block stands out as "a place to relax, feel comfortable, make sport, play games, gamble and have a good time."

On one occasion, members of the Gulf Massive reported having to flee for their lives after being attacked by over 30 men from Persian Gulf wielding cutlasses and guns. The Gulf Massive men suffered chops severe enough to require stitches. They also reported that girlfriends were also being singled out for revenge beatings.

The evidence clearly shows that warring communities are the result of simple, usually indeterminable misunderstandings, fueled by egos and allowed to escalate, often with disastrous consequences. The erroneous characterization of the term "disrespect" is almost always at the root of many of these conflicts. This is demonstrated throughout the book.

CHAPTER TWO

The Pine

History of the Pine

The Pine is one of Barbados' largest communities and the transition zone between rural and urban Barbados. It is located on the eastern fringes of the Bridgetown suburbs and has the lushness of the Pine Basin on its northern flank. On its outskirts lies one of the main arteries for traffic entering and leaving the City of Bridgetown.

There is however, the perennial perception by the Barbadian public and by some of the residents of the Pine area itself; that there exists a simmering slate of disquiet in the Pine. It has been stigmatised as a problematic community - an area one had to be cautious going into because of the temperament and aggression of the residents. This image of the Pine Housing Area has persisted to this day.

According to former Minister and resident of the area Hamilton "Hammie La" Lashley, there was the infamous PPP saying in the late 1960's and 1970's: Perry, (a Guyanese Magistrate working in Barbados), Pine and Prison. Perry would place all residents of the Pine coming before him to sit in a corner of the court, and there would be an almost guaranteed minimum sentence of three months' imprisonment imposed. Such was the level of prejudice to which the Pine residents were subjected.

The great flood of the 1940s

A lot of people came into the Pine area because of the great flood of 1948/49. People were moved from Halls Road, Martindales Road, The Ivy, Carrington Village and as far as St Lucy and placed into the Pine because of the dislocation caused by this flood. According to Mr Lashley, it created a cosmopolitan effect with people, dispossessed because of this natural disaster, from varying backgrounds and unknown to each other, being placed together in very close proximity. This cosmopolitan effect was later proven to be a negative one in the circumstances.

At the time of the flood, a new set of houses was being constructed in the Pine. While the entire project was not fully completed, some houses were sufficiently finished to be habitable, given the prevailing circumstances.

Unfortunately, there were no indoor facilities. The houses were built with outhouses - one had to go outside to use the toilet and showers. In Princess Royal, which is a part of the Pine, there were houses that had an upstairs (first floor) section, but the flooring was made of wood. These floors formed separate apartments, so the people living downstairs (ground floor) were affected by every single movement of those upstairs. It became a perfect recipe for conflict. In addition, there was no recreational facility for the early occupiers. The remnants of these houses can still be seen in Princess Royal Avenue.

According to Lashley, the lack of amenities and social infrastructure, coupled with the area's lack of a unifying identity, spawned the issues in the Pine community. This was also exacerbated by the 'cosmopolitan effect' of the transplanting of different communities there. People started to fight and quarrel and this created much internal strife and conflict, so much so that the police had to visit the community on a regular basis. As a result of being constantly called to quell conflict in the community, the police was inadvertently placed in the unenviable position of being labelled 'The Enemy of the People'.

How the war between the Pine and Chapman Lane started

Gang warfare is not new. In the early 1970's, there began a war between the Pine and Chapman Lane that lasted for three years, with its genesis as intriguing as a fictional movie.

The Parkinson Secondary School, located in the Pine, had an annual fundraising event in the form of a fair which had become highly anticipated and quite popular.

There was a young man from Chapman Lane with a mental disability who attended the fair and who, for no apparent reason, became the target of a merciless beating by some men from the Pine.

The severe beating of the Chapman Lane youth ignited the wrath of the people of that Bridgetown area. The men of Chapman Lane organized a gang as a response to that incident; the Pine Men did the same. Neither side wanted to involve the police – and so started the war which lasted for 3 years.

Hamilton Lashley makes the point that the Pine at that time was considered a lawless community. There were some bad men from the Pine, like Mackie, who had developed considerable notoriety throughout the island.

Mackie had a long criminal record. When Barbadians of that era heard his name, it was alleged that they trembled.

Chapman Lane also had its own bad men who were also feared by Barbadians.

Lashley identifies this war between the Pine and Chapman Lane as the largest and longest visible war between two communities on Barbadian soil. The war was so vicious that if you were working in Bridgetown or its environs (considered to be in Chapman Lane territory), and came from the Pine; or men even *suspected* you were from the Pine (women were exempted), you would be beaten! Many people started to deny that they came from the Pine for fear of retaliation.

The cinemas - Olympic, Empire and the Plaza - were all located in Bridgetown and they were also all frequented by the Pine Men. They who would come down from their community to watch movies, particularly on weekends. The men from Chapman Lane, armed with pieces of 2 x 4 wood, chains, ratchet knives and the weapon of preference – cutlasses, would reportedly come through the cinemas, particularly at intermission, with spotlights looking for the Pine Men.

Lashley recalled "From the time you hear 'One there!' the Pine Men would start jumping over seats and patrons and take off running for their lives! They would run from town straight to the Pine with men from

Chapman Lane running behind them. These groups of men totaled in some cases, ten or twenty men chasing the hapless Pine residents. And you had to run… and you had to know which gap to run through and hide so they couldn't see you. Many a Pine Man had to run to save his life during that war!" Anywhere the two groups were spotted, whether it was the bus stand, cinema, in Bridgetown, or on playing fields, there was conflict.

There was an incident when the Pine was playing a football game against Police Sports Club at Weymouth in the City. The Pine Men had a reputation as very skillful footballers. The men from Chapman Lane got word that the Pine was playing at Weymouth. From all reports, the Pine was winning, when out of the blue, about 30 men from Chapman Lane men invaded the pasture. As they charged onto the field, the Pine Men reportedly jumped over Queen's Park wall, ran into the Park, and then raced straight to the Parkinson Centre in the Pine, arriving there even before the bus that had been parked at the Globe Cinema next door to the Police Sports Club to transport Pine people back home.

The very next week, the Pine Men were playing a football match in the Pine. The Chapman Lane Men regrouped and the same group came up to the Pine with cutlasses, 2x4 pieces of wood, saws and hammers to maim any and every one they saw from the Pine!

But that was their mistake!

"They got brave and came too far in the Pine. They came on the enemy's turf," said Lashley.

The men from the Pine saw them coming up the Long Road, now known as the Pine East/West Boulevard. When the Chapman Lane Men got deep into the Pine territory and landed on the football pasture, the Pine Men retreated to the Community Centre and locked themselves in. Eventually, they stopped retreating.

That same day changed Chapman Lane Men from ever venturing into the Pine!

Mackie turned out to be the saviour on that day. Mackie was known as a man who dressed in trench coats with an assortment of weapons stashed underneath – weapons which he used to unleash his terror on unsuspecting persons.

Mackie had managed to get some dynamite from his father who was a well digger. In an interview with Mackie, he recalled that the Chapman Lane Men came up there to destroy the Pine.

This day in question, when he noticed the advance of the group of men from Chapman Lane, he quietly went inside, and donned his famous black trench coat, on which was inscribed the ominous words '**The Undertaker is here. RIP.**' Calmly enough, Mackie took out two sticks of dynamite and lit them!

It was reported that the Chapman Lane men started scampering for dear life - left right and centre.

Mackie ran the men out of the Pine!

Lashley recalled that after that, one or two of the Chapman Lane men wanted to prove a point and entered the Pine through Chapel Gap, went into a bar in the area, and started bragging that nobody from the Pine dared do them anything.

Unknown to them, some men from the Pine were in the bar and heard their loud boasting.

"Where are you from?" said one man in the bar.

"I am from Chap...," he started to reply.

"You gotta mean Chapel Gap! Cos you can't mean Chapman Lane?!" retorted the man from the Pine.

And a fight broke out.

Another incident occurred in the rum shop by the former site of the National Library, in Mahogany Lane, Bridgetown. The Pine Men would often go to the library to borrow books.

On the day in question, some men from the Pine left the library and went into the shop and called for two Pine Ju-c's. (A Pine Ju-c was a locally manufactured carbonated beverage with a distinctly pineapple flavor and colouring).

From the corner of the shop, they heard a man say "Call for another drink!". They ignored the man and repeated the order. "Two Pine Ju-C's." The man repeated himself. "Call for another drink!" What they did not realise was that this man was from Chapman Lane and took it as a serious affront for someone even to call for a PINE Ju-c. All of a sudden, two men flew out from the back of the shop and attacked the men from the Pine with two 2 x 3 planks! The Pine Men had to flee up Roebuck Street to get away from their attackers.

Indeed, the war entailed a whole lot of running, getting beaten and chopped, and minding strict turf restrictions.

This went on for a few years. It caught more than the public's attention. People got so tired of the war. They became tired of the skirmishes in the cinemas, on the playing fields, in the roads, in the shops; they became tired of having to run for their lives when the fights erupted in full public view. People were just tired and fed up.

The then Commissioner of Police, Mr Aviston Prescod called the two groups together at Central Police station. The leaders of the groups met under the watchful eye of the Commissioner and his team and the war ended right there.

However, that violent reputation of Chapman Lane and the Pine still remains in the minds of Barbadians up to this day.

When the Pine was at war with itself

Communities are often convulsed by their own internal conflict(s), and as if the horrific experiences of past inter-community strife were not enough from which to learn, the Pine still had some challenges within itself from which it needed to be liberated.

The Pine was at war with itself - tantamount to a civil war for about a decade. One block of people controlled one geographical precinct in the Pine, while another controlled another area. Invisible lines of demarcation were set out in the Pine. Within the Pine community, two different blocks were at war: the Dungeon block from Parkinson Field and the "Academics" block from Regent Hill. The men in Parkinson field could not go in Regent Hill and vice versa, without havoc being wreaked on the community. The internal war was about control of territory. Men who were considered extremely intelligent were formally established as leaders.

The older residents were fearful and felt terrorized and many residents could not sleep at night.

In June 2007, Inspector Stephen Griffith from the Royal Barbados Police Force went to then Minister of Social Transformation Hamilton Lashley, who was also the Parliamentary representative for the area and said something had to be done. They (the police) did not want to conduct any counterproductive, heavy handed interventions, but rather were seeking a harmonious approach to the cessation of the conflict. Lashley, Rodney Grant, a community activist and Director of the Pinelands Creative Workshop and Stephen Griffith went the next day and met with Academics in Regent Hill. Lashley referred to Academics as a highly sophisticated organization run by intelligent people.

They (Lashley and others) also met with the Dungeon block.

Both blocks agreed to meet together with Lashley, Grant and Inspector Griffith.

The Sunday afternoon of the scheduled meeting, June 3rd, 2007, Lashley recalled, resembled a western movie!

Peace pact between Dungeon and Academics in the Pine (Nation Newspaper, June 4, 2007)

At 1:00 p.m, the two warring groups approached the Parkinson playing field from opposite directions. The atmosphere was tense – the proximity of national elections adding to the tight atmosphere.

People on the sidewalks observing [the approaches of the warring factions] scurried quickly into their houses and then ran to the windows to peep out to follow what was going on. The opposing political candidate for the area, who was canvassing at the time, got in his vehicle, and beat a hasty retreat!

"The men of the two blocks were predictably hostile to each other ... chest pushed up and they were most likely armed," Lashley said.

Lashley invited them to sit down. They sat; they talked, they argued; they blamed each other for the war; they cursed each other. But Minister Lashley and his team told them that the war **had** to come to an end and "It ends today!" was the clear message of the team.

The two groups agreed that they would cease the war between them and that is exactly what happened. They kept their word.

"The leaders were strong, decisive and determined," complimented Lashley.

That same evening, there was a peace football match between the two groups, sponsored by the British Embassy. The war was officially over.

Shortly after the war was finished, the women from some of the Pine areas started to fight.

The women from Black Guerrillas (another block) and Wildey started to fight at football matches and other areas. It was alleged that the fights were over men. The fighting became so bad that many a football match came to an end because of these fights. It became so prevalent that the women had to be brought to a peace meeting. This resulted in the cessation of the war between the women.

For years, there has been no ongoing violence between groups in the Pine – happily, this continues to this day.

CHAPTER THREE

Historical Context Of The Gang Situation

Barbados has always struggled with the concept of gangs existing in the island.

In the 1980's, when the issue of gangs became a topic of national concern, Government Ministers, Attorneys-General, law enforcement and the general public were highly skeptical as to whether Barbados did indeed have gangs.

Successive Commissioners of Police, Attorneys-General and even the troublesome groups themselves publicly rejected the notion that Barbados was the home of several ruthless gangs, and depending to whom one spoke, these factions were referred to as "a loving brotherhood", "lawless groups" or "boys on the block".

Nation Newspaper, October, 1989

In October 1989, Minister of Employment, Labour Relations and Community Development, Keith Simmons went on record saying that there were no gangs in Barbados, this verdict being based on his not hearing of any gangs in Barbados who "[had] beaten people to a pulp" such as those in the United States.

Accusing the opposition of inciting mischief, Simmons suggested that both the Opposition and the Press were trying to create gangs by saying that they exist. His narrative was that it was all just an attempt to present the Government as incompetent.

Two months later, on December 6th, 1989 at the 90th passing out parade at the Regional Training Centre, Attorney General Maurice King was reported to have told the recruits:

"Whatever you do, don't get involved in sterile time-wasting arguments over terminology, as to whether we have gangs or mobsters in our particular jurisdiction."

AG King also criticized what he called Barbadians' penchant for using the "idioms of large metropoles". He told the recruits that their duty was to reach out to young people in the community and to recognise and understand the community problems which usually lie at the root of the crime problem.

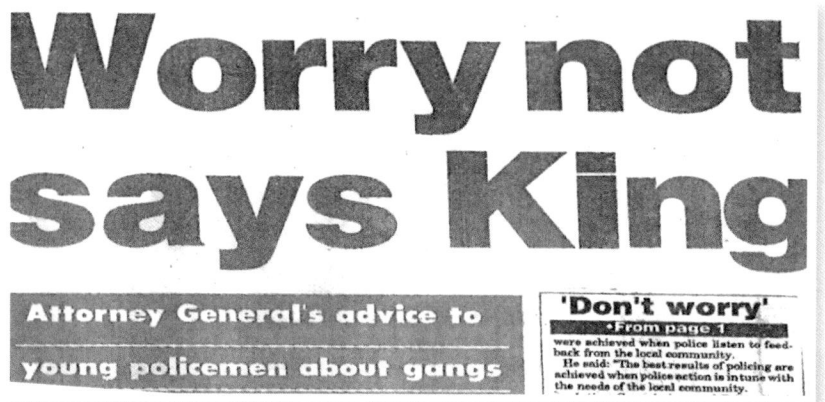

AG Maurice King's views on gangs, Nation Newspaper, December 7, 1989

Yet, unabated, the press continued to highlight that Barbados was experiencing a "gang" problem. Screaming headlines such as *'Gang roaming Neighbourhood'*, *'Boy hurt by armed gang'*, *'Gang Attack'*, *'St Philip Gang War?'*' *'Youth bullied, beaten by gang'*, *'Armed gang attacks minibus, injures visitors'* and several other stories about gangs dominated newspaper front pages in the late 1980's and 1990's.

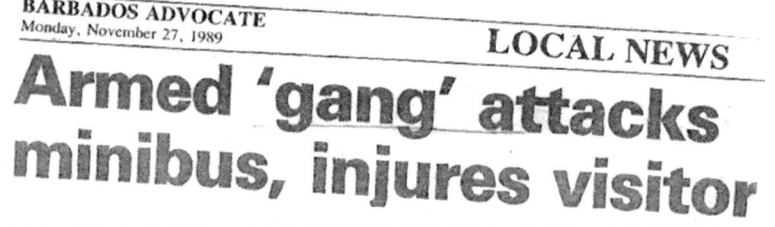

Media report on gangs, Barbados Advocate

Media reports on gangs, Nation Newspaper

The challenge was that authorities and the media were uncertain as to what to label them, and those labels were interchanged from 'gangs' to 'groups', to 'troublesome youth groups'.

Dressed to kill, but armed to the teeth

This was a headline in the newspaper, the *Investigator* in the early 1990s. Referring to men who frequented nightclubs at the time, journalist Sharon Austin wrote that these group of men would attend fairs and 'dubs', some wearing long coats. According to Austin, "however, while they may dance to a few tunes occasionally and innocently, under those coats, were weapons such as knives, sticks and cutlasses strapped to their bodies, in anticipation of a fight or spotting an enemy, whether it was an individual or a group."

Former Attorney General David Simmons, who at the time was the Opposition Barbados Labour Party's (BLP) spokesman on law and order, challenged the government's dismissal of these groups, publicly stating that he did not agree with Attorney General Maurice King.

Mr Simmons, (now Sir David) stated that Barbadians should not get bogged down arguing whether or not there were gangs, but must recognise the reality of the existence of these groups, their inducement of fear in the society, and that steps should be taken to root out the problem.

"My party's attitude to the present lawlessness is that we must as a matter of urgency have a national task force on crime and establish a Commission of Inquiry to find out why young people are behaving as they are. It is unscientific to apply guesswork to the causes of crime, because all have subjective opinions as to these causes."

In 1995, when the BLP regained the government, the National Task Force on Crime Prevention, now the Criminal Justice Research and Planning Unit, was established.

Fifteen years later, in June 2010 as the Penal Systems Reform Amendment Bill was being discussed in the Senate, Dr David Durant warned that it would be unwise to dismiss reports that Barbados had a gang problem and that any issue related to gangs should not be swept under the carpet.

"When I heard of the emerging gangs in Barbados, I know many tried to ignore it. For whatever it is worth, we need to give some attention to it. Some may argue it is being blown out of proportion. I will not go down that line, but for whatever it is worth, I think we need to give some attention to that gang problem that is within our society," Senator Durant said.

One month later, Magistrate Faith Marshall-Harris warned that the gang culture had reached the island's secondary schools. She referred to it as a "fairly new phenomenon with the potential to corrupt Barbados' school population."

Magistrate Marshall-Harris also shared information about what she learnt from young offenders coming through her court. She spoke of the operations of gangs such as the Crips and Bloods, believed to be two of the most feared gangs on the island at the time, as well as about other gangs operating on the island.

"I must say that I missed the signs for a very long time," confessed the Magistrate. Like most of the adults in the society, I did not actually accept that we had a gang problem. The point is that we are going to have to face up to it. They are here."

"No Youth Gang Crisis", says Stuart

The refrain was repeated by then Attorney General Freundel Stuart in June 2010, who was adamant that while some youths may be restless, youth gangs were not a menace to Barbados.

"I don't think there is this threatening gang problem in Barbados," said Stuart. "We do have some restlessness in certain areas of the youth population and a lot of it has to do – let's be very frank – with the despair that flows from the absence of access to employment and that kind of thing."

However, he admitted that law enforcement was monitoring the situation. "I don't think it is at the level where one can describe it as a crisis. I wouldn't be inclined to exaggerate the threat at this time. I would be inclined to agree with the [Anglican] Archbishop [Dr. John Holder] that 'yes', there are challenges out there, but not to be blown out of proportion."

If you don't know what they are, how will you tackle who they are?

What the media, and indeed the Government at the time, failed to do was to explain or define what constitutes a gang. Nor did either of them seek to have some technical authority explain the behaviours being exhibited at the time. Neither a definition nor a scientific explanation was offered; no strategy was given to tackle the problem appropriately and in the absence of specific directives on what exactly should be done with these "lawless groups", officials continued to play the guessing game for decades. Meanwhile, the 'problem' continued to fester.

Lack of gang legislation

One of the challenges to dealing effectively with gangs is the absence of gang legislation. In December 1990, Inspector Glen Gale who was Acting Public Relations Officer of the Royal Barbados Police Force stated that laws were needed to deal specifically with the problem of gangs in Barbados. He said under the existing legislation, the police could not do anything about gangs specifically. He said "If a disturbance is reported, we respond and deal with the situation as we would any other disturbance, but to deal with the gang situation in Barbados now there has to be clearly defined measures in place." Inspector Gale lamented that the police could only do as much as the law permitted. "Police need more authority in dealing with the gang situation," he stated.

He said to solve the problem of rising gang violence, all weapons made or adapted to cause bodily harm should be outlawed.

Over 25 years later, Assistant Commissioner of Police, Mark Thompson made the same point. Part of his interview is covered in Chapter 18, 'Evolution of the Streets and Gang Culture'.

In April 1992, with an aim to curb gang violence, Government stated that it would amend the 1970 Public Order Act, giving statutory effect to the common law offence of Affray and creating new crimes of Violent Disorder. The Act was eventually amended and proclaimed in 2002. It speaks to public meetings, processions, political meetings, protests and so on, however, it does not specifically address gang activity.

CHAPTER FOUR

The Culture Of The Street

In every society there is a strict code, specifically in street culture, where there are unwritten rules on how to behave. Some of these unwritten rules are:

- Do not snitch,
- Do not talk to the police
- See and don't see
- Protect your community at all costs
- Do not take any disrespect.

It also speaks to the use of violence as an expected response to being disrespected.

Barbados is no different. There is a code of silence on the streets of Barbados, where a 'kachar', or 'informer' (snitch) is the lowest form of life. Children are taught from very early that an informer is a reprehensible thing and that 'snitches get stitches'. The massive hurdle that adherence to such a code poses to criminal justice officials pursuing peaceful and just solutions, are all too obvious.

In some communities, to speak aggressively, swear and use verbal threats is important for establishing identity, but ultimately physical aggression is the expected way to assert oneself.

These behaviours are engrained and established by the time some children are teenagers. Research by ethnographers such as Anderson suggests that children growing up in these communities gain street knowledge at an early age. Many of these children gravitate to the streets even before they start school. These children have a great deal of latitude and are allowed to run up and down, unsupervised on the streets. This lack of supervision is usually due to several factors: insufficient or non-existent fundamental resources (financial), parents or guardians who are too busy or self-absorbed to effectively monitor the behaviours of their children or wards; an environment where these behaviours are accepted and normalized; and poor parenting practices.

On the streets, children observe just how conflicts are resolved through cursing and abusive talk and sometimes through physical aggression or violence. Children learn what they live. By the time they are teenagers, most young people have internalized the code of the streets, and have learned to behave in accordance with the code. From very young, one would see and hear the effects of the street culture in the behaviour of some young people; learnt behaviour through observation and expectations of the culture.

The importance of respect as a badge of honour

Respect, which resides at the very heart of the code of the street is taken extremely seriously. Elijah Anderson states that respect often forms the core of the person's self-esteem, particularly when alternative avenues of self-expression are closed or sensed to be closed. He opines that many persons residing in inner city communities feel that they are on their own, especially in matters of personal defence. The criminal justice system is seen as beset with double standards. and perceived as classist and even racist.

Anderson states that respect is fought for, held and challenged. As a means of survival, one often learns the value of having a 'name', a reputation for being ready, willing and able to fight or shoot. To establish such a reputation is to gain respect among peers. Having street creds, being known as a "Gangster" or a "Shotta" or even a "Boss" is very important on the streets. Going to prison is a rite of passage for many young Barbadian men in inner city communities and it gains these men street creds.

If one is assaulted or "dissed", it is essential for the street-smart person to retaliate in order to continue to have the respect of both his friends and opponents. If he is not careful, he can lose the respect of his friends, his 'soldiers' and even his enemies. To maintain his honour, he must show that he is someone not to be messed with or dissed.

One way to campaign for credibility, as is currently the situation of the streets in Barbados is to amalgamate gangs and crews

Another way to achieve status is to take other people's things and cause fear. So, a gun, a chain, a girl, someone's drugs, a Kangol hat (as what occurred back in the day), became prized possessions. Boldly taking away someone's things can symbolize the ability to violate somebody – to get in his face, to diss him – and thus to enhance one's own worth. Take for example, the CNN gang in the 1980's who boasted about its ability to take away drugs from drug dealers and chains from persons who opposed them. The ability to do these things gave that gang respect on the streets.

Many men from the street life crave respect to such a degree that they will risk their lives to attain and maintain it.

Walking away from an altercation is extremely difficult for the streets. It is likely to affect one's self esteem and even invite further disrespect. People often feel constrained not only to stand up and at least attempt to resist during an assault, but also to "pay back" – to seek revenge after a successful assault. Revenge may include going to get a weapon or even getting relatives and friends involved. Their very identity, their self-respect, and their honour are often intricately tied up with the way they perform in the streets during and after such encounters.

Anderson notes that the street code says it is better to be feared than loved. An old head or neighbourhood mentor may try talking to him and warning him what can happen if he does not change but as they said in most interviews, this intervention does little to change the trajectory.

The underground economy

Lacking trust in mainstream institutions, many turn to "hustling" in the underground economy. Growing up in such environments, young people are sometimes lured into the way of the streets and become its prey from an early age. For too many of these youths, the drug trade seems to offer a ready niche, a viable way to get by or to enhance their wealth.

Because the drug trade is organized around a code of conduct approximating the code of the streets and employing violence as the basis for social control, the drug culture contributes significantly to violence on the streets.

In addition, many inner city boys admire drug dealers and emulate their style.

Materialism

The drug trade, even though illegal, has become a way of life for many inner city communities. Many youngsters dream of leading the drug dealer's lifestyle or at least their highly glamorized conceptions of this life. The young man who sells drugs is often encouraged and motivated to create new markets, sometimes recruiting his own family members into the drug culture. (See Mario's interview in Chapter 6).

He had come to covet the material things he saw dangled before him, things that become important not simply as practical items but as status symbols among his peers. A particular brand of shoes or pants can indicate a person's social standing, bestowing on him a certain amount of self-esteem. The owner of these items, through his exhibitions and displays, is able to gain deference from and status among his peers.

Media images – television, movies, the consumer mentality fuel these desires as well. And when the regular economy cannot provide the means for satisfying them, some turn to the underground economy.

This encourages the development of the oppositional culture. For those living according to the rules of that culture, it becomes important to be rough.

The drug trade

The drug trade and its monetary returns are highly alluring and addictive. For some individuals, the opportunity for dealing drugs is literally just outside the door. By selling drugs, they have a chance to put more money into their pockets than they could ever get by legal means. Many young men get into the drug trade by being part of a neighbourhood peer group that begins by selling. Many drug dealers approach some of these young boys and get them involved in the business. There are those who are resistant to being drafted into the drug trade, but those who are drawn in are those who see very little opportunity to do well in the main economy.

Like any business enterprise, the drug trade requires a formal and well-defined structure. There is a hierarchy of power with the top, middle and lower order. The soldiers are usually there to protect the boss. The top includes the "real boss" – the person with means – financial and otherwise – to access the goods. This can be expanded to the gun trade as well. The middle man is the lieutenant who is more visible and who has his soldiers who protect him. The lower order refers to the soldiers who ironically are the first to die in any war on the streets.

Violence in the drug trade

Violence is an associated feature of the drug trade, not always intended but often occurring. Misunderstandings arise such as receiving bad or rejected product; not paying for drugs that have been advanced and thus squandering the dealer's investment; stealing another shipment from a rival group; cutting out the boss's profits and switching allegiance. These things cannot be countenanced; as to allow such, could result in the loss of credibility and status on the streets. The resolution to these problems is often the ordering of a hit on the perpetrator. Fueling these violent reprisals is the proliferation of guns, which have now become more easily accessible.

The drug trade is competitive and unforgiving. To mess up is to risk being beaten, shot or killed. Those who get into the trade know they are playing with fire, but given the financial stakes, many accept the risk/reward ratio.

Some boys crave the status and trappings associated with being a dealer or being associated with one. Drug and gun dealers are living in the fast lane; always on the edge. But everyone knows that once a person gets into that world, it is very hard to get out.

Guns and their differing styles and features have a graduated status attached to them. For many men, a gun is a symbol of power and it is considered essential weaponry for protection on the streets.

Some guns also have "hits" on them, meaning that they had been already used to kill someone. A gun with hits is not desirable because the person who is ultimately caught with it might be held responsible for any murders associated with it.

See but don't see

People residing in active drug communities understand the economic need for the drug trade. One man from a community in Barbados referred to it as a necessity and opined that it is a means of income for many 'ghetto youths'.

Many residents are aware of what is going on right under their noses. Many become disillusioned, yet they try to coexist with the scourge, rationalizing that the men who deal drugs are not necessarily bad boys but are simply doing what they think they have to do to make money. They themselves do not want to be victimized by the trade, nor do they want their friends or families harmed. Many have come to believe that the police and public officials don't care about their communities, and as a result they often say nothing to officials. The Robin Hood phenomenon helps the justification process. Some dealers try to assist their communities by donating behind the scenes to various families and friends towards noble causes like education, food and the improvements of general living conditions; with drug profits.

Another reason for seeing and yet not seeing drug transactions is fear. Concerned for their own safety, people do not even want others to notice them witnessing what is going on. After an incident like a shooting or a gang war, people tend to clam up for fear of retribution, especially when the police become involved.

Parents, family and loved ones also see but don't see for another reason: they realise that their own loved one is involved in drugs and organized crime. They may disapprove of it, but they also benefit from it. A mother, for instance, who receives money, sometimes even large sums of money, from her son may not ask too many questions about its source. She just accepts the fact that the money is there somehow. Since it may be sorely needed, there is a strong incentive not to interrupt the flow. Some girlfriends and siblings even boast about how much drug money they have spent in their lifetime.

Violent death

The streets have taken the lives of hundreds of young Barbadian men, in particular. The men who have chosen this life, have grown accustomed to unspeakable violence and have been witness to levels of serious carnage and often death, to the extent that some have made their peace with death.

Justin, who is interviewed later in this book, speaks about accepting that he would die a violent death while he was a gangster, and preparing to die with guns blazing.

After experiencing the death of so many of their friends or acquaintances, they naturally conclude that their life is bound to be short.

And such is the life of the streets.

CHAPTER FIVE

Defining Gangs

As we systematically peel back layer by layer of this unspoken and often denied issue of Barbadian gang culture, some questions need to be addressed before we get into the meat of the matter. What is the difference between blocks, crews and gangs? Are they all the same? If not, are there similarities? What are the differences? Can a block or crew be also a gang? Are all blocks or crews involved in criminal behaviour?

Barbados has always had a problem of armed groups of young men from different districts who choose to settle their differences with violence.

It is a fact is that gang violence has been on the increase in the region since the 1990's. However, not many sociologists and criminologists have chosen to undertake extensive, in-depth research on gang activity in Barbados and the region. Research into illicit or illegal behaviour is an undertaking fraught with danger, due to the obvious inherent threat of physical injury involved in such an undertaking. There is also another difficulty which presents itself, that of obtaining valid and reliable information from those who may either be involved in or are aware of such activities. (Nation newspaper, February 28th 1999). Investigative strategies have to be adjusted and new alliances forged, which becomes time consuming and resource depleting.

There have been however, a few notable studies and we will look at some of them here.

Roy McCree, a senior research fellow at the Institute of Social and Economic Research at the University of the West Indies in 1998 conducted a comprehensive study entitled *'Gangs In Trinidad and Tobago'* in the area of Laventille in Trinidad and published the findings in the Caribbean Journal of Criminology and Social Psychology. He defines "gang" to mean "a particular group of individuals or collective possessing some common aims and values, which might be formally as well as informally organised to engage in certain activities which can be deemed illegal or unlawful."

Former Research Fellow in the Centre for Public Safety and Justice at the University of the West Indies in Jamaica, Horace Levy, pointed out in his 2012 paper *'Youth Violence and Organized Crime in Jamaica; Causes and Counter-Measures'*, that the definition of criminal organisations, referring to gangs in Jamaica was very broad.

"It is so broad that it can include what we call 'defence crews' — groups of youths in communities that are not in the top number one or two groups the police have identified. They are not organised to rape, carry out assassinations, trade in guns and drugs, or to commit robberies. They are there to protect and defend their communities, and our fear is that that broad definition of criminal organisation is broad enough to encompass that.

"They are there to protect their communities, they use guns, they kill, they should be prosecuted, but they are not criminal gangs in the same sense as a Shower Posse, they are at a different level, and you can't treat that level in the same way."

An expansion upon this concept of 'defence crews' will be undertaken a little later in this chapter.

His research, done with the Institute of Criminal Justice and Security (ICJS) research team, was able, through focus groups and interviews with key informants, to engage directly with gangs and crews in communities in Kingston, and to a lesser extent, those in Spanish Town.

The team encountered "defence crews" that were aligned to communities. These crews did not exhibit behaviour of illegal, wealth-seeking criminal gangs and, indicated no movement in that direction. Instead, they were strongly supported by women and responded positively to the mediatory and developmental "best practices" of state and non-state agencies. A significant number of criminal gang members also showed interest in pursuing an alternative and legal lifestyle.

Some have suggested that a block in the Barbadian context is just a space for liming and relaxing. Blocks may be involved in illegal activity such as smoking and selling marijuana, but generally they are not a violent grouping.

A gang, however is an organized grouping with a well-defined hierarchy and structure which engages in criminal activity.

Since the 1980's, the residents of many communities in Barbados have lived with gangs involved in either violence or trafficking in cocaine and marijuana. These rival gangs have also been known to engage in armed conflict over territory. To control or occupy a turf means to have a physical space/base from which to sell drugs (to residents and others from outside the community), to give shelter, to use to hide and escape from police and to recruit members.

Gangs also do provide some minimal social benefits to the community, such as funding some social projects and events and even render assistance to some individuals.

Research by authors of books on crime in the Caribbean and Latin America note that the Don (the boss), who recruits these young men, is seen as a force bringing order to the community in the absence of effective governmental services and authority. (Barker 2005). The young men in the neighbourhoods perceive the Don as providing a useful extra official justice system that intervenes in cases of interpersonal conflicts and/or domestic violence.

Residents tend to view these bosses with a mixture of fear, dislike, respect and admiration. The members of these gangs are nearly all from the community, and while most residents oppose the violence, they also side with 'their boys' when violence breaks out between a rival group or with the police.

Whatever recognition is ascribed to these groups, one thing is for certain – they have brought, and still do bring a reign of terror, fear and destruction on certain communities and to Barbadians on the whole.

Media reports on gang warfare were prevalent in the 1980's and 1990's. CNN, Beirut, Lebanon, Vietnam, Dog Pound were just some of the names that were synonymous with an alarming rise in gang activity. Crime started to increase and the situation in Barbados became so dire, that the US State Department slapped a travel advisory on the island Barbados in April 1992.

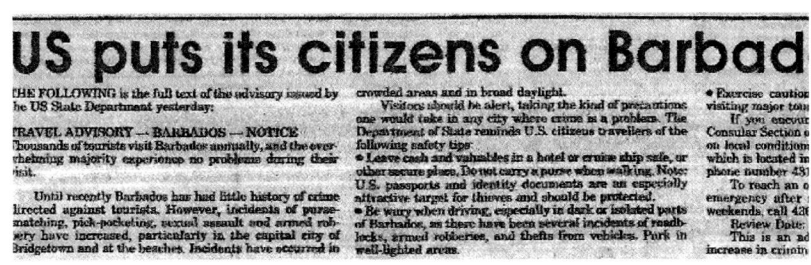

At the centre of the gang wars were feuds that had started with simple arguments between individuals from different communities that later exploded into all out gang conflict involving entire communities. Drive-by shootings, shootouts, choppings and stabbings between warring factions in public spaces were commonplace.

It resulted in the loss of many lives, destruction of property and the incarceration and loss of productive years for many young men.

With the May 1991 arrest in Trinidad of wanted Barbadian Don Grazette for robbery and shooting at policemen, the Barbados Advocate reported that same month of a Trinidadian gang link to Barbados. The story suggested that Barbadian criminals who were wanted in Barbados fled to Trinidad, where there was an established agreement between gang members to arrange harbour of such fugitives. Trinidad's hilly terrain was reported to provide security to the gangs there.

A police source told the press that wanted men escaped the island via boats and not the airport which was considered much too risky. The source also stated that all types of illegal items including firearms and drugs were being peddled between Trinidad and Barbados by gang members.

The police force was unable to identify the connection between the two islands but admitted that they knew that drugs and firearms were flowing between the islands, with Barbados being mainly on the receiving end. It was also suggested that the hilly terrain in the southern Caribbean island provided security to the gangs there. However, the police in Trinidad said that they could not confirm any of this and was generally unaware of any such inter-island links between criminal elements and their activities.

According to the Advocate, fishermen in Barbados at the time admitted that they were being approached to be part of the gun-running and drug smuggling activity between the islands. The newspaper stated that some of the Trinidadian fishermen were doing a brisk trade with those rackets.

In 2016, in a study done by the Criminal Justice Research and Planning Unit on Gangs in Barbados, the Royal Barbados Police Force (now the Barbados Police Service) stated that there were gangs all over Barbados in both urban and rural areas.

"They are not only islandwide but they are increasing!" asserted one officer.

Coming out of the research, it was noted that most gangs are made up of very young people. From the age of 15 years and sometimes younger, adolescents were frequenting the blocks. This younger demographic was considered to be a result of older gang members taking a back seat regarding gang activity. Some recruited younger members to do the actual criminal activity. Some older gang members retire altogether. One of the main contributing factors for making such a retreat is due to the older gang members starting families. "It changes them; they get out because they do not want any harm to come to their children," said one police officer. This reason was also given by gang members from *Thug Life* and *CNN* as is documented later in this book. That unfortunately does not happen all the time.

Local research states that gangs use guns not only to protect their turf and drugs, but also to establish status on the streets. Gang members would use fetes to "buss shots" to let rival groups know just how extensive and menacing their arsenal was. "Nobody ain't coming around men with a piece. When you packing, you are a king pin. Without it, you aren't saying anything. When war come, you must defend yourself!" was how one young man from the street life put it.

Organised crime is a complement to gang life. One police officer pointed out that the organized gangs were "the thinkers. They are involved in money laundering and have businesses as fronts."

It is believed that some organized crime is linked to corruption where there is infiltration of the criminal element into certain government institutions and even private sector businesses. "Illegal firearms are smuggled through any point of entry where persons in that capacity can be bought", said a senior police officer. "Corruption is very dangerous and deadly." This is an ominous threat to the system of justice and the rule of law in any country.

In 2016, the Royal Barbados Police Force publicly acknowledged that Barbados does indeed have gangs. The definition of gangs from Trinidad and Tobago's Anti-Gang Act 2011 was adopted. This Act defines a gang as:

"A combination of two or more persons whether formally or informally organized that through its membership or through an agent engages in criminal activities which are associated with gang-related activity."

Even though the police has acknowledged the existence of gangs, there are still some officials that continue to deny that these groups are gangs and just refer to them as troublesome groups.

Seeing the gang situation as "serious", many stakeholders believe that the problem is "not being adequately policed as it should". Some have referred to the gangs as "sleeping cells that at any moment can act up."

Definition of a gang

The UN Convention on Transnational Organized Crime, Article 2 defines a gang or "organized criminal group" as follows:

> "a group having at least three members, taking some action in concert (i.e. together or in some coordinated manner) for the purpose of committing a 'serious crime' and for the purpose of obtaining a financial or other benefit." It speaks to the aspect of these collectively committed criminal or delinquent acts, creating and imposing fear and/or intimidation to secure the intended financial gain.

According to the UN, the group must have some internal organisation or structure, and exist for some period of time before or after the actual commission of the offence(s) involved.

It also states that a **gang:**

- may have in common an identifying name, leader, de facto claim of territory/division or colour
- may or may not be identified or linked by visible markings or mannerisms; and
- may share or enjoy the proceeds of crime as well as conceal such proceeds.

Based on this definition, gangs have been in existence for years in Barbados.

The US Department of Justice (1997) notes that a youth gang is commonly thought of as a self-formed association of peers having the following characteristics:

- a gang name and recognizable symbols,
- identifiable leadership,
- a geographic territory,
- a regular meeting pattern and
- collective patterns to carry out illegal activities.

Youth gang members are actively involved in drug use, drug trafficking and violence.

A loosely organized gang gains cohesion as a result of a perceived or real threat from a rival gang. A mobilizing event then occurs, followed by an escalation of activity, a violent event, and rapid de-escalation. The cycle is completed when the other gang retaliates for the inflicted harm, creating a feedback loop in which one killing justifies another (Decker, 1996; Decker and Van Winkle, 1996).

Defence Crews

As promised above, I will here look at a special type of gang, not usually considered when exploring this area – the defence crew.

> **We are not a gang but...**
> **We will defend ourselves, say Silver Hill youths**

Silver Hill youth deny being a gang,
Weekend Investigator May 3, 1991

In May 1991, the Greenfield community and that of Silver Hill were embroiled in conflict. Greenfield was sending messages to Silver Hill that their residents were "banned" from entering Bridgetown or leaving their homes at night. At the time, Barbadians were referring to the conflict as gang warfare.

The residents of Silver Hill rebutted by saying that the definition of them being a gang was misleading – they were just protecting themselves as a group of residents, after being attacked in their own area.

One Silver Hill resident made it abundantly clear. "We are **not** a gang and will not attack anybody, but as long as a group makes the first move at us, we will retaliate to defend ourselves."

How the 'war' started

The men from Silver Hill recalled the time when a man from Greenfield was staying at his mother in Silver Hill and had "set up" a Silver Hill man into a position where his jewellery could be stolen. According to the men in the area, they heard of the plan, and approached the Greenfield man at his mother's house to find out if there was any truth in the accusation.

In fright, the Greenfield man called his partners in the city claiming that he was attacked, and according to the Silver Hill residents, that is how the mini war started.

Persons in the community decided to keep their doors closed at all times, particularly the older residents, but the younger persons would not be intimidated.

At the time, the police warned them not to go into town, but they were adamant that they should be able to walk freely in any part of Barbados.

"We are not scared. I have been to town every day by myself, and some of my partners have to go to work. It will be chop for chop, if they try us!" declared one resident.

"We are no gang, but we are together as one if trouble happens to come along.

"We have never been in anything with the Greenfield men before. It was they who roused us. We have always been quiet," said one rasta man. "We will never start a fight, but we can't go anywhere bare-handed now, in case we are attacked," another man stated.

Unfortunately, there occurred an incident when a Silver Hill man who had gone to the Globe Cinema with a group from his community, had to be hospitalized, after being chopped up by a group of men from Greenfield.

Not us!

On the other hand, the people from Greenfield were adamant that their community was being unfairly tainted and they were tired of it. One resident said, "This sort of foolishness has to stop because the innocent people from out here are being blamed for things that people from outside are coming in here and doing."

(Picture compliments Nation Newspaper)

While admitting that it was not the most ideal community, one resident said the old stains are hard to remove and far from being attackers, residents said they were often victims of violent attacks.

"We just have people from all about who come down here to hang out and do all sort of bad things." The resident said that whenever the police come looking for someone who they allege lives in Greenfield, no one knows them.

Alienation and discrimination

While claiming that they have to contend with unfair publicity about their district, they say they face a bigger problem – that of discrimination.

They reveal that they are discriminated against especially in jobs. One woman said she braided hair but her clientele had been reduced because no one wanted to come to Greenfield. "Even my friends are afraid to come here to look for me," she lamented.

So serious had the situation become, that many people who live in Greenfield are forced to give their addresses as Gills Road or Roebuck Street in order to avoid embarrassment or other problems.

Based on the definition of a defence crew given by Levy, it is fair to state that examples such as the one given above will place these groups into a defence group and not a gang. There are many groups wrongfully labelled as "gangs" in Barbados that are in fact, defence crews.

The following stories are based on interviews with former gang members in Barbados.

IN THEIR OWN WORDS: STORIES FROM FORMER GANGSTERS IN BARBADOS

Being raised in the subculture of drugs and violence

For many young people, the manifestation of violence is a part of their daily lives. Their environment places them in a subculture where they witness it, live it and are expected to respond to it similarly. Criminologists have sought to explain this using the subculture of violence theory, which essentially says that there is an expected way to behave as part of the street culture.

The following are interviews with men who have lived the gangster life. Some of them have now quit that life and turned to Christianity; some have just decided to move on due to age, but are still involved in drug selling and some are just dormant.

CHAPTER SIX

From Gang Life To Christ

The role of religion

Some ex-gangsters decided that they would rather be soldiers for Christ, than street bosses and have left the gangster life and, most likely, saved their own lives. Take Shawn, for instance. Shawn, an ex-gangster who converted to Christianity, gave an interview to the Nation newspaper in 2010 in which he stated that he was on a mission to transform the lives of current gangsters. Stating that he was now a man of God, he revealed that he had had a rough life growing up and that had been one of the reasons he joined the gang, which he had been a part of for more than 10 years.

He said in the interview:

"My mother was a domestic worker and I didn't have a father or father figure. So I didn't grow up with that guidance, and that is what a lot of the youths are growing up without."

Shawn also spoke of growing up seeing his sisters being sexually exploited by other relatives. This has stayed in his mind for many years. Referring to it as "mental abuse," he said he had since forgiven the relatives.

The ex-gangster, who admitted to going to prison several times, said that he joined the gang at 17 and specialised in robbery. He spoke about the rivalry with other turfs. "We had 'beef' and war with other turfs – about three or four other gangs. We used to roll up on them and shoot at the men.

"The men used to roll with nine-millimetres and Glock 40s and .38s. I wasn't involved with drugs, but robbery was my thing and I had this theory that God put me here for them sort of people who think them real cruel. I felt like I was invincible, like nothing could touch me."

He disclosed that there were hit men on the block that would "honour" the boss and the boss would send them to kill because he was not going to do it himself. "There had a hitman on the block and he died at 17 years old. His job was just to shoot and kill people. The last time he did a killing, the next week he got killed," he recalled.

"We could get a gun for $5,000 depending on the type. The gangsters on the street have guns just like what the police have," he claimed.

It was while incarcerated, that he said he took time to reflect on all he had done.

"I am telling this story for the other young people out there; to show them that God changed me. If God could change me, he can change them. But they have to want to change too.

"I think God put me in jail for a reason - because of the way I was rolling. God had to slow me down that year because I was on a fast pace; and he put me there to work on me. Maybe if I didn't go at that time, I would have gone at a different time for a bigger charge – maybe murder or something; or maybe someone would have killed me."

He told the media that he had quit going on the block and had stopped smoking and was waiting on God to direct his path.

Adorned with tattoos on various parts of his body proclaiming *"Bad man"*, *"Thug for Life"*, *"Black Jesus"* and *"Fuck the World"*, Shawn now wishes he could remove every last one of them. Referring to them as "openings for demons", he said he got them all anointed with oil.

He warned the gangsters on the streets, "It is a life no one should aspire to live. Don't take it up. Don't start. Don't even look at it. I have friends that are dead and some doing long prison terms because of gang activities. It might look sweet because you smoking and rolling with guns and with people who you think have your back. But at the end of the day, if you are not one of the lucky ones, who you think have your back then?"

INTERVIEW WITH MARIO

Mario is a former gangster who sold drugs on the streets, a lifestyle that he was born into as his father was also a drug dealer.

Mario strongly believes that the gang and street culture is one that is handed down from generation to generation. Being exposed to that lifestyle increases a child's chances of adopting that lifestyle. As a young boy in primary school, he was aware that his father was part of the drug trade. He also saw the profits and benefits derived from it. And from an early age, he knew he wanted to emulate his father. He remembers, as a young boy around the age of seven or eight years old, seeing his father smoking in the privacy of their home. He would ask his father for a pull of the joint, and his father would oblige him. Mario revealed that it wasn't long before he started smoking marijuana to the extent that it became part of his lifestyle.

Mario describes his childhood as one defined by poverty and hardship. In fact, he makes the point that to escape the grinding poverty was one of the reasons his father became involved in the drug trade in the first place. His father had established connections in foreign countries and would traffic marijuana into Barbados by boat into specific landing areas.

For much of his childhood, Mario's father was not around, and he holds a lot of personal guilt about this. He recounts an incident which occurred when he was still a young boy.

One day when the entire family was at home, there had been a knock on the door.

"Who is it?" Mario had asked.

"It is the plumber," the person on the other end of the door had responded.

Mario had no reason to be suspicious. After all, there had been issues with their kitchen sink, and living in a housing unit, he had thought that the National Housing Corporation had sent a plumber to fix the problem. Without looking outside, Mario had opened the door only to be confronted by a squad of police officers who had swarmed the house on a drug operation.

He recalls his sister sobbing as the police found a quantity of marijuana in the house. Both his parents had been arrested and placed before the courts. Mario said that both parents had received a fine, with his father receiving the heftier amount.

Mario believed that if he had only looked through the window, he would have prevented his parents from being arrested. He carried that heavy guilt with him for a long time as a young boy and developed a resentment for the law. He believes that this is what brings the hostility and conflict between the police and 'ghetto people', especially the youth – the trauma of seeing their mother or father or others in their community being arrested. It creates an anti-system, anti-establishment mentality, and a deep detestation of the law and anyone and anything that represents it. According to Mario, one develops and cultivates a mentality that opposes the law, such as selling drugs and being involved in the gun trade.

Mario stated that his father, unable to pay the fine, fled to St Lucia where he developed a relationship with another woman and began another family. He would be back and forth on a boat from St Lucia and even came into Barbados by plane on a St Lucia passport and was never identified by the law!

Meanwhile, without a father figure, Mario looked to the streets to fill that void.

Mario became addicted to marijuana. Admitting that the addiction steals your potential as a youth, he said that he and his school friends saved their money to buy marijuana. School began to lose all appeal and meaning for him. He became very delinquent. "I spent a whole promotion term away from school. I became disinterested in school because of my addiction to smoking. I started to see myself as a man and not a child."

He said he would just go to school and lime with his crew; they would be involved in bullying younger children, gambling and buying the biggest portion of marijuana and smoking after school in shanties which he and his crew had built together.

"We would sometimes steal bags and break and enter businesses," Mario revealed.

He also witnessed his mother get into abusive relationships after his father absconded to St Lucia. However, because of the community he came from, some of these abusive men were beaten within an inch of their lives by other men in the community.

Mario eventually dropped out of school at 14 years old, blaming drugs and a hard life at home for this decision.

After dropping out of school, he started cutting lawns. He also connected with a man who was established in selling drugs. Mario and his friends would lime on the block and ensure that they fit in with the older, more experienced men – the 'elders'. These elders saw in these younger men the potential to be part of the 'organization'. A special link between Mario and an elder, who was into selling drugs was established, and Mario began to sell drugs for this elder.

It was at this time that Mario and his brothers grasped that their father wanted to pass on his inter-island drug trafficking business to them and allow them to become 'drug bosses' themselves. He noticed that Mario was now selling drugs on the streets, and his intention was that on his next trip to St Vincent, he would put some product on the boat for Mario.

However, the dangers inherent in drug trafficking would soon come to roost at their home. Other persons seized the product, and Mario recalled strange men from overseas came looking for his father. "The deal went sour," said Mario, "and someone had to pay."

Never saw his father again

Mario recalled that day he last saw his father. His father was heading out to St Vincent on a boat and asked him to use his sim card, as he did not want to use his own. Mario never saw his father again. It was rumoured that he had been found dead in Vincentian waters with a bullet to his head. Mario vividly recalled that there was a very small article inside the newspaper, mentioning the incident.

The body was never retrieved. But instead of using this tragedy as encouragement to get out of the drug business, it only strengthened Mario's resolve.

Volatile at-risk communities have the decks stacks against them. Growing up, young people are subject to the pervasive influence of music and music videos, all celebrating violence. There are criminal and gangster movies glorifying the criminal and gangster life. Compound this with the abject poverty and lack of education and, thus, opportunities; the antisocial behaviours of persons in these communities: and men hiding drugs and constantly running from the police. Mario stated that in his community, he saw even six year olds running from the police. It was a culture inculcated in their minds from a very young age - to be against the police.

Meanwhile, Mario became more and more involved with selling drugs on consignment for the elder man. The arrangement was a convenient one, and once one wisely retailed what one got wholesale from the elder man/the boss, one could make a healthy profit. However, in Mario's case, although he was able to pay back the boss his money, he would smoke all of his own profit, causing him to make nothing!

But it is not lost on anyone the vast amount of profit that can be generated by the drug trade and this proves an irresistible lure to many youth marooned in poverty and seeing no other route to access the coveted "Big Life."

With the real possibility of attaining such massive sums of cash, it is inevitable that human greed will enter the scenario.

Mario notes that in the past, the drug pusher would not sell to children. However, nowadays, the drug pushers have no such qualms. According to Mario, they do not care where the money comes from. In Mario's words, they are "bolder and lack any form of moral conscience."

"Young boys and girls, 11 and 12 years old, are going to the pusher man and buying drugs and cocaine. The generation on the block is much younger with children selling children drugs nowadays."

There is no doubt whatsoever that human greed spawns a great deal of gang wars and loss of life on the streets. For example, two drug bosses would agree to land and split a quantity of weed, and then the boss who does the actual landing decides to keep all for himself. A gang war would ensue.

Inter and intra gang/block relationships

Wars between gangs are prevalent. Many of the conflicts start over petty arguments that escalate to violence - robbing or tricking another street man with drugs; even high words can cause a war. This can have a ripple effect.

Even though between gangs, there is hostility, there is also camaraderie. For example, CNN and Jesus and the Disciples forged alliances. They also shared product.

Mario did speak of the camaraderie within the crew itself – the feeling of being part of a family. For those who lacked this in their homes, the experience of this element on the block increased the attraction of that space. He explained that there were different levels of camaraderie. There are those relationships that are extremely close – where you are each other's 'dawg' – willing to risk one's life for the other, or to seek revenge on those who would have disrespected your 'dawg' in some way. However, Mario also stressed the volatile nature of relationships within the crew. Today, you could be roasting breadfruit with a man and tomorrow you and that man could be at war. And these wars could erupt from many things. Sometimes, men may *trust* someone's weed and take too long to pay back; sometimes a man borrowed someone's gun or took someone's motorcycle and did not return it; sometimes a man was talking to another man's woman. There are others within that crew that if you make the wrong move, you could be killed because they are not as close-knitted. **Gangster life is a very unpredictable life** and people start dying, left right and centre," Mario explained. Many gangsters have to live a life looking over their shoulder.

"When the crew became established, we would be hailed up on the radios by DJs and on the street", he said. This empowered the members. As the block became more established, and drug trafficking became more prevalent, the elders also provided the younger members with guns.

When probed as to why they were provided with guns, two main reasons were offered: One - to protect the boss (as his foot soldiers) and two - to make them – the soldiers – feel secure. Security and protection are crucial aspects.

"If really as a crew, and there are 2 or 3 guns among the group, you can match with anyone!"

"Men on the streets need to feel protected because a threat is always imminent. They feel that they need weapons just in case. For example, a day like Kadooment Day, you are not looking for trouble, but you must arm yourself because it is possible that something can happen and you will have defence."

Some of the men on the block lived to prove themselves as a shooter or to prove their loyalty so that they could win the trust of the boss.

Referring to the streets as a "dark game," Mario implicated persons from all strata of society in all roles, including law enforcement. Admitting that he had access to bullet proof vests while on the streets, he said that the reality is that "there is a lot of corruption out there."

Foot soldiers:

Foot soldiers exist to protect the boss. Admitting that he was once a foot soldier, he recalls that some nights they would be outside surrounding the boss's house or even in the bushes, while the boss was inside making love to his girl. That was the nature of the game – absolute, unequivocal loyalty to the boss.

Mario believes that young men are mere pawns in the game of the streets while the bosses live lavishly.

"Young men dying or incarcerated are collateral damage. They are not the source of the drugs. When a man goes to prison, he is not the source, not even near the source. The source is still supplying; making sure his soldiers eat and are content. If the boss gives you two pounds of weed to keep you in his arms, to make you feel like 'This man cares about me', that's what matters to them. It is all about materialism. Rolling around in two or three cars makes them feel wanted. They see this as the big life," he explained.

"The bosses have a lot of young men around them. Most shooters and killers would kill you for their boss."

According to him, the established gangs or crews recruit young schoolboys. Mario stated that if one looks closely in schools, one can see who has a crew mentality and is heading to gangster life.

He admitted to witnessing a lot of violence and even a few murders – a lot of blood while on the streets. He remembers one occasion being at home and hearing a volley of gunfire. When he rushed outside, and down an alley, he saw two men on the ground mortally wounded. That, he said, came about from a *scene* where a man popped another man's chain.

He recalled witnessing his friend getting shot in his chest while in a club.

He and his friend had attended a backyard party and while coming through the entrance to the party, they passed a group of men. One of the men stepped on the toe of his friend.

"Big man, you step on my foot!" exclaimed his friend.

"So what?" was the man's response.

The challenging disrespect was received and a fight arose.

What they did not know was that the man had a gun on his person. Mario heard an explosion, screams from the patrons at the party, and then there was a wild stampede. His friend was holding on to him when everyone started to run, but in the ensuing confusion, they lost each other for a brief moment. When they reconnected, his friend told him that he had been shot in his foot, but on closer inspection, Mario realized that there was blood dripping from his friend's upper body! The gunman had shot him in his chest and punctured his windpipe! Mario's friend was rushed to the hospital, and miraculously survived. While Mario is no longer part of that life, he said his friend is still actively involved in the street culture.

Seeing a lot of violence, especially in one's environment will naturally impact one's own disposition and response to conflict. According to Mario, "You always have a mentality about warring; this is how you have to live your life." Even going to fairs and parties could mean coming into conflict with different blocks, resulting in throwing big rocks, stabbings and shootings. Seeing that violence in one's environment and being told by your family or elders to strike back, "that is the mentality that you have as young people when it comes to violence." But as the wise saying goes, "an eye for an eye only leaves the whole world blind."

He sought to explain the upsurge in school brawls being witnessed in Barbadian society. "It is about dominance and ego and not looking soft" in front of one's peers.

Mario is strongly against giving murderers bail and wonders if there is a sinister reason behind it. "Does the system know what they are doing when they give murderers bail?" He is convinced it is leading to a lot of revenge killings.

Gun out fetes

"Gun out fetes" are also part of the street culture. This is when men go to fetes and openly carry guns while there. A group of men would be together with the boss in the middle, surrounded by men with guns in their hands. This open display of weaponry creates tension in the party and according to Mario, the men "come with a vibe". They walk with these guns to prove that they are a dominant force and no one can step to them. It gives them status and recognition; it is meant to proclaim "We are the most dominant force on the streets in Barbados."

The gun-lyrics music in these fetes, in his opinion also helps to feed the mentality of violence. When he was living the street life, he was a big fan of 'Black Kartel" when he would sing violence. He would smoke and meditate while listening to these songs and identified with the lyrics in the songs. "Our hearts were sold out to this violence," Mario said.

Facing death

"How will you feel if you wake up one morning and saw
a big M16 nozzle at your jaw.
Feel like you waan disappear, but you can't.

What will you say if you're coming from dance and you red
Hear a voice say boy no move or else you're dead
When you take a look fi see a who from far
It's a boy weh you and him a war

Certain boy haffi go plea
Beg fi dem life and go down 'pon dem knee
Certain boy haffi go flee
'Cause dem know if a did dem
Dem would no have no mercy

Beenie Man from the song "Murderer"

As stated earlier, gangster life is very unpredictable and the harsh reality is that one can be killed at any time in that lifestyle. One day, in the middle of a gang feud, a gun was put to his head. "I felt helpless, weak and fearful… just having the moment to see and think this is the end," Mario recalled.

"I wouldn't wish it for anyone; feeling the iron of the cold nozzle, pressed against your head and telling yourself this is it!"

But according to him, God had a plan - and the man did not shoot him and he lived to see another day.

Exiting the gang and street life

Mario was asked what made him get out of the street life. His candid response: the day that he experienced Jesus Christ.

At the time his friend was shot, Mario had been employed for 9 months. His plan at the time was to buy some guns to avenge this shooting.

One day he was home cleaning and smoking a joint when he came across a book called *'Steps to Christ'*. Mario began to read the book. It was about repentance and confessing one's sins. As he read, the words resonated within him. "Lord, I hope you know what you doing. It is life or death for me." Mario repeated a prayer in the book and cried out to God, "Please forgive me of my sins." That was the beginning of his conversion from a life of crime to a life for God.

After praying to God, he said the addiction was broken.

"God is real. He can change the trajectory of a youth's life if He is given the chance. I had 16 years of addiction," he said.

He used to smoke 10 – 15 joints a day and God took away his addiction.

Mario remarked that marijuana now smelt like mosquito coil to him and that he had no desire or taste for the drug.

He was invited to a Bible study and he said God kept him employed. He is now married with a child and is now an ordained evangelist.

"God changed my life and I believe he can change the most violent killer. Jesus can change your life," he stressed.

After giving his life to Jesus, he remembers traveling on the road one day and encountering a man from a group who had wanted to war with him in a prior shoot out. His first reaction on seeing this man was "All this Jesus thing, you have to fight now!"

To his surprise, the man said "Wait, wuh gine on?" and knocked fists with him. He was amazed.

"God took me out of war, and changed the mind of those against you. It had to be God who made that man change his mind against harming me," he said.

Interestingly enough, Mario does not believe that the solution to the prevalence of gang violence is merely giving young unemployed men who are living street life employment. "You will just make them independent gangsters," he warned.

"You need to find other ways that we can feed our minds," advised Mario. The youth today need to consider there is a God."

He now lives free and does not have to run from the police or look over his shoulder against any gang violence.

"This is the best life!" he reiterated.

CHAPTER SEVEN

The Life Of Ken – A Dormant Gun Man

Ken is a former gangster who was the boss of a 'crew' in urban Barbados in the 1990's and early 2000's. In an extensive and wide-ranging interview, Ken spoke about growing up on the streets from a young age.

He admitted to smoking marijuana from primary school while living in the Pine and Chapman Lane. Growing up, he saw men abusing drugs and alcohol all around him, and was curious as to how these drugs would affect him.

"I saw men smoke marijuana and stood firm and still held their sanity, but I saw men smoking cocaine laying in the gutter and begging people." He vowed he would never touch cocaine.

When he was 11 years old, his father told him that it was time to teach him what a father is supposed to teach his son. Thereafter, he moved into Chapman Lane to live with his father, and that is where according to him, he "learned life".

Parental knowledge of his lifestyle

He admitted that he had not been interested in being a bad man, but when he went to live with his father in Chapman Lane, he saw "how the men move." His mother realised the change in him when he used to return to the Pine to spend time with her. When his mother would complain to his father that he was rude to her and did not have any manners, his father would merely laugh and do nothing.

Initially, his father had no idea that he was a gangster. One day, when he was sitting next to his father, he phoned his best friend and crew associate Ian, on the phone and told him, "Tell my father who is me! Tell my father what they call me on the streets and who I really is."

Ken handed his father the phone and Ian then told Ken's father his (Ken's) nickname and shared that Ken was in charge of the known crew.

His father laughed in disbelief. "Yea right," he said.

Suddenly, Ken took two guns out of his waist and placed them on the table in front of his father.

Shock enveloped his father's face.

Ken recounts that his father went deathly quiet, put down the phone in Ian's ears and just stared at the guns and then at Ken. He could not believe what he was seeing and what he ultimately had to come to grips with – his son was a gangster.

"How long were you into this, son?"

"This is just how I keep it Daddy," Ken had responded.

""I heard about this crew, but I had no idea that it was you," his father began. "Just be careful son," was his father's astounding reply.

Like his contemporaries, Ken believes that the young gangsters of today are very different from his time.

"Youngsters nowadays have no respect for me and you. We would say 'Yes, please,' 'No, please,' 'Yes, Mummy, Daddy', 'Good morning,' 'Excuse me.' I was a big man and a gangster and my father dragged me home [unknowingly] with a .38 [gun] on me. I running the gang, but gone home like a little puppy with Daddy, because he reprimanded me for not carrying out the garbage!" he recalled.

His mother knew he was running a gang, but when he was in her house and his mother gave him "badism talk" he kept his mouth shut. On the streets now, it was a different story! "If I outside and you make the slightest mistake and take out a knife, I would put you in the hospital!" he warned.

Ken recalled an incident where he had chopped up a man. His mother had asked him about it. "Mum, he was out there quarreling with me, and he owed me piece of money and giving me talk, so I just chopped him up and done." His mother's response was to hold her head and say "You are crazy!"

One has to ask a few questions here:

Were his parents enablers? Were they afraid or did they choose to ignore his involvement in gangster life? Were they beneficiaries in any way and afraid to lose these benefits?

How Ken learned about the streets

In Chapman Lane, Ken would come out on mornings and see the men selling drugs on the streets. But Ken also made the point that the Don of the day also played another important, more positive role in the community.

He referred to the Don as a "very good man" to the community. Ken thought of him as a role model and as a young boy, he idolised the Don.

"If your electricity was off, he would pay it for you and the arrangement was you would repay him every month.

"He brought the young men together and started football teams," said Ken.

The Don was protective of the youth in the community and would not let anyone "unfair the youngsters." He would look out for his soldiers and make sure that everyone was fine every week.

The Don then, was considered a leader in the community.

Ken recalled that when he was younger, he had been involved in a confrontation with a man named Stephen. He was going to complain to his father, but another man in the community had taken him to the Don. The Don had told him "Pick any man to beat this man [Stephen]!" Ken had then chosen a man named Jackman who beat Stephen really badly.

"Don't ever tell your father about this," the Don had commanded him. Ken obeyed and never repeated the incident to his father.

Years later, when Ken was now a grown man, he became friends with Stephen's brother, Robert.

One night, Ken was in the *Front Line*, a former party spot, selling weed, when his supply had run out. Robert, who knew of the incident years before between his brother and Ken, was at the same venue and told him that his brother Stephen had weed. The prior incident had never affected his relationship with Ken.

When Ken arrived at Stephen's house, he said he went to him and "rest my .38 in his belly" obviously to intimidate him.

"You know me? You remember you hit me?" Ken asked Stephen, who looked most confused. And then the light of recognition came on!

"You is Ken?" The man quickly apologized.

However, Ken harboured no ill-will as he felt satisfied that Stephen had paid for the past incident when Jackman had beaten him.

"I ain't come to do you nothing. I come for an ounce of weed," Ken had assured him and the purchase came off without any violence.

Life as a gangster

Ken started his crew in the 1990's while he was still in his early teenage years. "We started as friends that just linked up. It was nothing planned."

He said when he was 19, he had men in his crew who were in their 40's. When asked why he had men so much older in a crew with him, he said "It is a vibe."

As Ken became older, he began to gain access to guns and marijuana and realized the power of owning a gun. But it is interesting to note what Ken considers to be a gangster.

"A gangster is not a man who breaks houses or steals or snatches bags. He is a man who knows how to deal with people, and how to handle people in any situation.

"Even the police liked me. They knew that when I was rolling, I wouldn't just snatch anyone's bag. If you in the Pine and snatch someone bag, and I hear about it, you mash up. If someone goes in a woman's house and takes away something, and I hear about it, you lick down. So because you with me and moving with me, don't feel that you stealing. I don't deal with that stealing thing," he said.

He remembers a time when he went with some men to Redman Village and two of his men decided to rob a man at a bus stop. He was riding a bicycle and passed the man at the bus stop crying. He stopped and asked the man, "Big man, why you crying so? You woman left you?"

The man said no; that some men had just robbed him of his money - $350.00. He said he had children at home to feed, which hurt Ken. The man described the robbers to Ken, who right away realized who they were. Ken told him not to move from the bus stop. The man asked him if he was going to the police. He told him, "No, don't move."

Ken went to the identified men, who were members of his crew, and asked them who had taken the man's money. One of the men said he had it. Ken told him that he had to give back the man his money.

"I don't rob and give back!" the man responded.

Ken said to him, "You don't rob and give back? Ok! Well, you will give back now though…or you will rob and bleed. You have a choice."

Without further ado, the money was returned to the man. Simple like that.

Learning the streets at a tender age

Ken also relates the story of his very good friend, Ian.

His friend, Ian, has been Ken's best friend from his boyhood days. Ian later became a soldier for a notorious gangster who is now deceased. Ken said he 'brought him out' when they were mere boys, about 10 years old and living in the inner cities of Barbados. When Ian's mother left home, Ken would get his brother's clothes, put them on Ian and he and Ian would go into town. Ken "taught him town and taught him places." He recounts how, on one occasion, while they were in town, they saw Ian's mother! Both of them fled and ducked through an alley and went home before she got back home!

Ken revealed that he had taught Ian life and things he had to learn on the streets at that tender age.

"Ian didn't know Chapman Lane or other places in the City nor did he understand street life, so I schooled him."

Respect on the streets – power in numbers?

Shortly after Ian had left Chapman Lane, he got into a 'scene' with some men from the Pine. The men from the Pine 'had talk for his friend and tried to test him and 'stepped around him'. Ken went to defend his friend - his '*bredren*'.

"I told him 'Let we go down in there!' I had a sword and he said he had a sword too. I told him bring a knife, too! Then we went for the men!

"It was just two of us but a block full of them. Ian showed him who was who and he drew his sword and "stick it around the man's head." The men started to fight and throw rocks and according to Ken, Ian started to get 'active'. "I told Ian defend himself and he started to mash up men."

After that incident, Ken said a few other friends started drawing back around him and they all started to feel more comfortable. When they had gone out alone, people would try to challenge them, but "when they in the platoon, it is respect." People would know they are a part of the [named] crew and "don't step to them."

Difference between Ken and other gangs

Ken notes that at the time, other gangs started to step out – Egypt in Carrington Village, CNN in Tudor Bridge and Beirut in Carrington Village. He said he would 'roll' differently from those men, and even current gangsters. In his opinion, these men were greedy, self-absorbed, and looked to take from other gangsters; but he was different.

For instance, if a man came to him and said "I get 5 kilos of dope," and came and showed it to him, he would not take it away. "Error! I will try to show him how to make the money. If he wants a buyer, I will get a good buyer. If you get money, control your money. If you give me 10 cents from it, that is your thing."

This, he asserted, inspired and deepened his team's loyalty toward him. "There was no red-eyeing. Because I am chief, does not mean I want to unfair you and take away your things. If you bring in a gun, I wouldn't want to take it away from you. That is your gun. If you have weed and dope and can't get it sell, I would make a connection that you can get it sold, even in these times that I am holding it down."

He said even now if a man wants anything, he calls him. "If a man wants a gun, he calls me. Even though I am holding it down, I still get that respect.

"If I see one of my men have something, I don't try to take it away because I know it can bring vibes. The Bible tells you if you have eight friends and eight enemies, and you make your eight friends your eight enemies, what have you gained? As I said earlier, as a gangster, you have to know how to deal with people. Because a man bring in he thing, and you brek and you have nothing, you shouldn't go and take away his thing and he is one of your soldiers. You are giving him a motive now to get you hurt or killed."

He remembers getting in a *scene* with a man who had a mock gun. He pawned the man his chain and when he came to pay the man for his chain, the man told him he liked the chain and was not returning it. Ken said he took his chain from off the man and told him to hold his money he had brought. The man left and returned with a gun wrapped up in cloth. Ken said he stopped talking, because the man had a gun and he, (Ken), only had a cleaver. While the man was talking, Ken "threw the cleaver around his head," and knocked him out. He stepped on the man and took the gun out the bag and pulled it on him and squeezed the trigger. It was then he realised that it was a mock gun! He then hit him again with the cleaver for coming around him with a mock gun.

"You can't sport people out here, because they will kill you. Men will kill you out there for nothing."

He said he knew of cases where men did wrong things and blamed other men and the wrongfully accused man got the bullets and was killed.

"A man would go do something and it is not you and call your name, and a man would kill you just like that and then hear it wasn't you."

Jail's life lessons

A stint in prison opened his eyes. He said it taught him and conditioned him for the men on the streets. Referring to it as "a blessed place", he said it showed him how men really are:

How they crumble, how men are unjust and deceitful; and in some cases how stupid they are. It showed him how men move, how men smuggle things. He learnt how to be always aware of his environment and of everything that happened in it. Prison taught him more about the streets and how to operate on the streets, about men engaging in homosexuality etc.

"A man would get 10 years and come to prison and talk about everyone's car, every one's girl, talk about their crimes – things considered unimportant," he said.

Ken admitted that at one point, he was a functioning illiterate who could not even spell 'cat' at primary school. However, in prison, he got books and educated himself, so that when it came time for him to reason and articulate, he could do so to anyone in any social setting. Knowing that he was not able to read, he said, he fell in love with a dictionary and started to learn and spell words.

He said people from Brittons Hill thought he used to smoke 'blackies' (cocaine and marijuana mixed together) because he would treat them mean. They thought he was not normal and had to be "on something," because of how he would behave. He said he knows that men smoke blackies to get high, but he would listen to calypso and chop you up. He did not need blackies!

"If I in a scene with a man and I have a sword, knife or gun, I looking to treat you vicious. There is no coming back for me. If I don't kill you, I looking to put fear in your heart. You is to check yourself when you come back round me.

"I could go on any block right now, and who don't know me, if they hear my name, will know me. I went places that Pine men couldn't go. Wherever I go, it's full respect."

Yet, he revealed, some of the men he had around him who he thought were loyal, were actually enemies. If the police came and asked them what gun he had last night, they would tell the police what gun he (Ken) had, how many shots he had sold, to whom he had lent a gun, etc. And the police, who is supposed to be the enemy, would then relay to him what his man said about him. He did not know about men *kacharing*, (men informing), and for that he gave the police respect.

"I was the stronghold for the Pine because I was about unity. I pick up some of everybody from every block, because wherever I go, people wanted to be a part of me and my crew.

"I chopped up a man with a sword because he violate. A fellow pelt a bottle and hit me and got away. A night I saw him at the Caribbean Broadcasting Corporation (CBC) at an event. I ran home and took up my sword, because the most I used to beat was a sword or a knife back in those days. I still had a firearm but the firearm was the last resort. I wouldn't land on no block and attack you with a firearm. I would chop you up first. Most men nowadays have a sword and a gun, but would take up the gun. They don't have balls."

Ken identified the man in CBC by his shirt. However, what Ken did not know was that someone had swapped shirts with the man. "So I was watching and focusing on this shirt, not who was wearing it. When I started to throw in the chops, the man looked around and I saw I had the wrong man. I told him, 'You have on the wrong shirt, boy!' War doesn't have rules!"

Police came the same time and he was arrested.

Ken's views on the current state of the streets

Ken laments the difference between the gangs of old and those of today.

"Right now how the streets are running, the youngsters say they don't care who is who. They don't care who has a name or who used to do anything. So, if I have respect for a youngster coming up but the youngster says he does not want respect from the old ones; that is easy. I don't have respect for them either."

Ken is of the view that the older gangsters, unlike the younger ones, had some morals.

"Nowadays the youth do not care where you come from. There are men that are gangsters, but they are not bad boys. They can't deal with badness. They can't chuck the badness thing. So when a man come for them, they paying money to get you killed; they giving the youth guns to protect them because they are frightened for their own skin."

Paradoxically, Ken claims he lives by the *Book of Proverbs* in the Bible, which teaches you about wrath. He says that he is dormant now, but warns that, like a volcano, he can very easily erupt and be quick to retaliate if threatened.

CHAPTER EIGHT

Kool And The Gang

Some Barbadians from in the 1970's would recall a group called Kool and the Gang, which originated in the Wavell Avenue, Ashdean Village area of Black Rock, St Michael. Its leader's name was Freddy, diminutive in stature – about 5' 5" – and was described by those who knew him or came into contact with him as a tyrant with a propensity for great violence. The youngest and only boy of his mother's three children, Freddy himself fathered 11 children. He referred to himself as a "wicked man" and made it clear that he is not a man to be messed with.

Freddy attended the St John The Baptist school up to the age of 15. He admits to fighting at school, and to "pelting through the school at a teacher," who hit him with a bamboo for pitching marbles. He hit the teacher with two big rocks and was suspended for a few weeks. When he returned to school, the teachers were fearful of him and did not want to work with him. Freddy took up his bags, went home and never went back.

After he left school, he started selling hangers in Swan Street and started a life of hustling.

How the name Kool and the Gang was derived

Freddy revealed how his nickname 'Kool' came about. The moniker was thrust on him due to his typical response to the greeting he received from the men in Brittons Hill, where he frequented. "When I used to go up there [in Brittons Hill], the men would shout 'Ah, short man! You good?' And I would say, 'I cool,' and simple like that, the name started from there." The American musical band 'Kool and the Gang' was also popular at the time.

Earlier actions of Kool and the Gang

The grouping was initially about six men, the oldest being about 20 years old, but it grew in number when men from other areas such as Chapman Lane chose to link up with Freddy.

According to a retired police officer, the group would assemble on a bridge just before Ashdeane Village and cook a large pot of food next to the road. This pot fed the group and even other residents of the area were never denied a serving.

Some of the members of the gang engaged in petty criminal acts such as theft, and purse snatching.

"We had to hustle as a gang, because none of us was working," Freddy explained. He maintained that they never broke into anyone's house. However, while they did not break into people's houses, Freddy said supermarkets in the area would give them produce for free, not because they were being generous, but because they did not want them to break into their businesses. He would go to the door, and say that he wanted something to cook, and they would give him the items.

The gang served as some sort of protection, because other criminals or shoplifters could not go into the supermarkets in the area. "If they went and thief, we couldn't get anything to cook," said Freddy. It was a symbiotic relationship.

He also revealed that there were imposters pretending to be Kool and the Gang doing crimes, and as such his group was blamed for a lot of things that it never did.

War between Kool and the Gang and Sly and the Family Stone

A war started between these two groups of men stemming from an altercation at Ellerslie School when someone from Freddie's group called a man from Grazettes a homosexual and conflict started from then.

Freddy, aka 'Kool' and his friends retaliated and according to him, it was then that they started to be referred to as *Kool and the Gang*.

As Freddy tells it, it was the Grazettes men who started the war. Freddy says it was one 'Phil' from the group *Sly and the Family Stone*, which was a fairly large, marijuana-dealing group from Grazettes, who decided to come down to Lower Black Rock and look for war – "So they got war!"

Freddy related that he and Phil had a previous altercation at the Sandy Lane Golf Course where he had almost cut off Phil's hand. Phil had '*chucked*' Freddy not knowing that Freddy had a sword hidden in the sand pit! Freddy also disclosed that he had stabbed a man named Chris from Grazettes. So bad blood already existed between Freddy and the men from Grazettes. The Grazettes men would come down to Black Rock and fight, and they in turn would go up to Grazettes and bring the fight to them.

After the war started, the Grazettes men could not come down to Black Rock, and had to find alternative routes to get anywhere they wanted.

The war lasted for a few months. It resulted in many choppings and stabbings between the two groups.

However, the war started to wear down the two communities. It was then that Bobby Clarke, who was Freddy's lawyer at the time, said that the best thing to do to end the war, was to get the two groups together and shake hands and make it a media story. After much discussion and interventions, the two groups decided to end the conflict. They shook hands and agreed to end the war between the two groups

Freddy constantly stressed that he was a 'wicked man'. He admitted that he would provoke people with insulting comments. As if to emphasise his point, Freddy also displayed numerous scars of stabbings and chops that he received. At one point, he said that he could not walk for three months due to these attacks.

Freddy recalled a time when a man named Colville pulled a gun on him and he hit him with a big rock, and then took a sword and chopped him. Colville had to be hospitalized and Freddy was charged with serious bodily harm.

He was also charged with attempted murder twice and was remanded. He has three convictions.

Freddy confessed that while he had pulled a gun once or twice, he preferred to chop his victims because, in his words, "I like to make them hear!"

Hustling

He admitted that while in the 1980's, cocaine was not as prevalent as it is now, they would sell '10 plays' and '20 plays' which was a small piece of cocaine stone, put into a pipe and smoke.

Even though he does not use drugs or has never 'retailed' drugs, Freddy would send people to sell drugs.

"I am not going on the block, but I would send men on the block. I was always into selling drugs **wholesale**! If I get drugs, I would call a boy and say 'Yea, I got X.' I would sell direct to you if you come to me and say you want a pound, but I would not go on the block. I had to hustle. I had 11 children to support."

As to whether they were a gang or not is unclear, but at the time one thing was certain – Kool and the Gang drove fear into Barbadians, particularly those from the Black Rock area.

The gang, however, did not last long. Police disbanded Kool and the Gang by executing a search warrant one morning. All the members were picked up and some were charged. The gang never reassembled after that.

CHAPTER NINE

The CNN Gang

The *CNN* gang originated in the urban community of Tudor Bridge, St Michael sometime in the mid-1980's. It had about four main bosses. Three are still alive today, but one named Peter Rabbit died at sea in 1994.

Exclusive interviews were conducted with members of the *CNN*. They explained how the gang developed, the structure of the gang; the activities in which they engaged; and the events leading to the murder of one of its members in Sheriff's Place.

Most of the men interviewed are currently fathers and grandfathers. One of the gang leaders said that even though it had been the four of them, three of them "did the most damage".

How the name CNN originated

There is some discrepancy regarding the origin of the name. One leader said it was because the group knew a lot of things. According to another leader, people in the neighbourhood would have the habit of taking news about the gang's activities in the community, to the media. Because of this habit, he had written the name '*CNN*' in the road, indicating that the people in the gap were "real malicious: dem like *CNN* news."

At the same time, journalists from *The Investigator* newspaper came to uncover the story of this gang, as it was becoming a topical issue, and according to this particular leader, on seeing what he had written in the road, the journalists remarked, "Oh, it's *CNN* gang". He said "this sound good," so he affixed the word 'gang' under it. And that, according to him, is how the gang *CNN* was formed.

From then, they started attending fairs and stoking fighting at these events. "We just loved fighting," he said.

The *CNN* was known as a gang that terrorized several communities and the general society, with residents living in fear. Indeed, some 30-plus years later, just the name '*CNN* gang' still drives real fear in the hearts of many who remembered this gang from the late 1980's and early 1990's.

According to two of its original leaders, John and William, the gang started under a tamarind tree in the community and most of its members were no older than 22 years of age. They lived as a brotherhood, and cooked and 'limed' all hours of the day.

"We were like a family; a real family back in that time," said John.

John remembered that Peter Rabbit was older than he, but he – John - would control the gap. He and Rabbit were close and would spend a lot of time together. "When I was younger, I didn't really move with them, because they would break shops. They grew up breaking shops before there was even a *CNN* gang."

John left school at 14 because the Principal wanted to beat him and he told the Principal he was not taking any licks. He worked as a labourer at various jobs. He would come to the village where he lived, and would cook and go to street jams, where according to him, "things would start," and they would get in "little ends of fights and people would get chopped up."

He was asked why they always had to walk around with weapons.

"When you leave your turf and you are going someplace else, always prepare for the unexpected," he said. "The *CNN* would always prepare themselves in case something happened, and you wouldn't have to look for anything and you would end up having to defend yourself."

He said people had such respect for the *CNN* gang that other gangs or groups would pay them to come on their turf. *Jesus and the Disciples* was one such gang. The *CNN* "felt their energy" and let them into their gang. They were one of the few that they let in. He claimed that many came and brought money to buy guns, for instance, and they made a lot of money in the gap because people just craved being a part of something that was going on and to associate with some well-known group.

In the later stages, as they became bigger and more established, they would sit around a table and do things differently. They would have discussions and target men; when they heard a man landed weed, they would plan how many of the men would go for him.

"All cannot go for him - all can't get tie up. You always leave back someone to help. You have to leave someone to push the buttons when that man wants to lock you up, you have to push his buttons to dun that," he said. By this he was suggesting that there always had to be a negotiator on the outside (not incarcerated) to threaten/encourage the victim to settle or drop the case. "You have to go to the person who wants to lock you up and offer them something. You have to dun the case.

"When you go on people's turf, there are people who would see you and don't like you," he said. Girls, for instance, would go out with them, and if the girls were dancing and were approached by men who are persistent, this could result in conflict. "That is how war would start."

In an interview with Matthew – another member of the *CNN* – he explained that Barbadians were afraid to come in that community and some people still are afraid 30 plus years after the *CNN* disbanded. "The *CNN* name still carries a lot of respect," he stressed. "People still are afraid to come down in there," he said.

He believed that this was a good thing because, according to him "If you come down in here doing foolishness, you will get treat rough."

However, he preferred to bury his past and uplift the community through positive vibes and "downbeat the *CNN* stigma."

Drug running

John admitted that he would do drug runs back in the late 1980's.

Drug run to Canada

John and his friend left Barbados on a flight to go to Canada with 4 kilos of cocaine each - some was strapped on them and some was liquid cocaine.

At the time, he was wanted by the Barbadian police for robbing a man who they were told had a lot of cocaine in his possession. The man however, tried to attack them with a collins, and they had "gun-butt" him several times.

When questioned as to how he was able, as a wanted man, to get out the island with cocaine, his matter-of-fact response was "because you got ways…and everybody likes money."

There were no scanners at the airport at the time. In the Departure Lounge, he was pretending to be reading magazines, but he was checking around to see if anyone would approach him. No one did, so everything went smoothly.

When he and his friend were on the plane, he recalled a Vincentian businessman involved in banana export, who was traveling for the first time. The man sat between them, and his friend kept telling him not to let the man touch them, because the man was afraid of flying and extremely nervous. He kept fidgeting with his tie and was sweating profusely; he was asking a lot of questions and kept touching them. They were very anxious that this man would bring unwanted attention to them and blow their cover.

When he landed, he said the lady at Immigration asked him what was his purpose for entering Canadian soil. "Right now, I am on holiday and I heard about the country and I come to sightsee and do some shopping and she gave me a stamp for 6 months." According to him, "She didn't know what she was letting in, but she let me in."

When he arrived in Canada, he was given a big gun and $10,000.00. He sold cocaine on the streets in Canada. He spent two years in Canada, and lived well, he said, even though the last year was spent in prison. He received a plea bargain and was deported to Barbados.

Drug Running - England

John and another man also went to England to do a "job" for a man who owned a store in Bridgetown. If someone paid him to go and do a job, he would have done it back then. The recipient of the drugs in the UK did not know him, but all he really needed was a picture of the person and knowledge of the assigned meeting place. John saw it as a straightforward, relatively risk-free transaction - he would go, "do [his] work" and come back.

He went to England to live for a while, but spent a year in prison there for gun possession because "I don't take talk.

"I would do what I had to do and go back inside and watch television," he said. He had to have a gun because he sold cocaine and it was for protection. "If you confront me and I don't know you, you will bite the dust."

One of his former henchmen migrated, but he too, was caught selling cocaine abroad. He referred to his friend as a brave man who liked training. He would go on the beach and exercise because when committing crime, he "had to have wind (conditioning) all the time."

"If you are not fit, no matter what you do, you will be out of wind. A good criminal always has to be fit."

"If you want to do things, and you aren't fit, the police will hold you, because when you run, even if you fight with someone, you will see that you are breathing heavy... you have to put down that body before five minutes. It is all about fitness – crime is about fitness."

Pack mentality

"We used to move like how werewolves would move – in a pack. We would move together because we were raised in the same neighbourhood, the same ghetto," said John. However, he said they were neither troublemakers nor bad people, though the police branded them that way. He tried to diminish their behavior by saying that they would get involved in certain things and people would get hurt – according to him "mash up," but the police did not see it that way and considered them troublemakers.

When asked how they got involved in wars with rival communities which led to men dying, his explanation was "People want to be more superior than others and people want to outdo you in certain areas, so that is the reason why people die."

William, another former member said that they would go into the Globe cinema and walk through town, drink alcohol, and break up bottles in the streets. "Then we started targeting gay men and would run them through town. It was fun for us," he recalled.

When a church came under fire

John recalled that while bathing one night, his cousin had come to him, telling him that a fellow from *CNN* and a group from Bush Hall were fighting.

"The men now run somebody," his cousin told him.

When he got outside, he asked the other *CNN* men where the men had run to. He was told by his cousin that the rivals had gone into the church.

"And wunna here standing up?" he had shouted angrily.

"And that is when I 'pull through' the church. I pull big rocks through the church. I have a very short fuse. I don't take no talk, nor want no talk. If you come in my space, something will move you," he warned.

According to him, the men retaliated and he turned them back and went back for them, "because you have to do things."

"You can't take a downfall, and then when you gone, people will be at you and say that you weak. You have to retaliate because men will feel that you are soft."

William recalled how he became involved in gang life. According to him, he was having issues with his son's grandmother and he "burst the grandmother's head with a case of bottles." He was charged and placed before the courts. The Magistrate banned him from going around the house and seeing his son, and fined him $500.00. According to him, when he tried to explain himself, the Magistrate still proceeded to stop him from seeing his son.

This "played" on his brain. All he was thinking about was the fact that he could not see his son.

Robbing drug dealers

"I was going mad. I told Rabbit (Peter Rabbit) 'I have to fight this out. Leh we go in the Greenfield and tek way all de big pusher men weed'.

"We start with some .38's and start with Greenfield, Chapman Lane and The Orleans. The men start asking themselves 'Who is dese two lil men?' They start hearing about Rabbit and William, Rabbit and William.

Rabbit was a person that people feared, and according to one of his friends in the *CNN* gang, even those in his family feared him because he had a violent temper.

That started their reign of terror where they started "taxing" drug pushers.

"The pressures of not seeing my son was sending me mad." Others took up his energy and started fighting too. "We tear up real people in Barbados: that's how it was," he boasted.

They would break into shops and rob people, something they had done from very young. He admitted to terrorizing taxi men in the 1980's.

The younger men from the community then emulated these older men and the *CNN* gang became divided into the younger boys and the men in their 20s. The younger men would rob minibuses and other vehicles. Other gangs would also come and 'lime' on the *CNN* block because they wanted to "move with them" – Jesus and the Disciples from Shop Hill, St Thomas, and other gangs craved the fame that came with the association with *CNN* gang. Men who had started liming in the area, would commit crimes and say they were from the *CNN* gang.

Even though there were three leaders, each leader had his own friends. "We would go to fairs and just fight with anyone that wanted to fight". They would fight with collins or machetes. According to him "we didn't have no lot of guns in dem times. It was pure chopping up and stabbing up. That's what I did like."

He also hinted that it was easy to get away with murder, but never admitted to actually committing any.

When asked how they got their guns, which they did not use often, he said they would either buy them from the weed men or take them away from them.

The use of extortion - "taxing" the drug dealers

While the youngsters were robbing minibuses, the older members of the *CNN* gang were operating on a bigger scale.

"We would drive around and target certain groups, particularly drug dealers, and tax them. When men landed weed, we would tax people and they would bring out the weed, even if it was just a pound." He claimed that he had the first motocross in Barbados. This motocross had emblazoned on it *"**CNN Sick Ass**"*. He also had a big gold chain with the same affixture. "When men heard my bike, they knew the CNN Sick Ass coming."

The gang would also make the drug dealers pay them not to attack/shoot them, or for protection. "Give me something when I pull up if you don't want me to shoot you," said William.

According to him, they targeted the drug pushers because they had children to support. "When we left home, be guaranteed we were coming back with something – weed, dope, money, anything".

One member of the *CNN* tried to downplay and even justify this extortion. "If we hear you have 'something,' we would roll up on you, come and sit down and talk to you. People would call it taxing but when we talk with you and you feel our energy, you would give we something and that is how we used to roll," he said.

He strongly justified the extortion used by the *CNN*. "If a man land 1000 pounds of weed, and he has to give you 100 and something pounds of weed, that ain't hurting he." When it was explained to him by the author that this was indeed extortion, he said "we didn't see it that sorta way then."

He claimed that they hardly had to use violence to tax people because of the *CNN*'s reputation.

Even though people were scared of the *CNN* gang and did not want to pass through the area, he maintained that they never interfered with anyone passing through.

However, he admitted that he "did dirt" (engaged in wrongdoing) and would take away the chains of rivals from different communities if there was any conflict. He boasted of his 23 convictions, some for shooting people, wounding, grievous bodily harm and an assortment of other crimes, but stressed that he never went to prison because, in his words, he had a "top lawyer" who knew people. "I always heard it is who you know," he laughed.

He sought to explain why they were not a gang, but a family. He said they moved together as a group and were all neighbours. In his opinion, Barbadians thought they were a gang because if you interfered with one, you interfered with all. "When we go out, don't come in that pack and give trouble. You can come in, but don't give trouble. If you give trouble, you would get lift out of it." When asked to clarify that statement, he said, "the ambulance would have to move you."

The gang was considered so ruthless that when reggae artistes came on the island to perform at shows, they would act as their bodyguards.

Many incidents of lawlessness, fighting and the use of dynamite as weapons were linked to the *CNN* and other gangs.

There was an incident in December 1990 at the Victoria Sports Club, St Philip where dynamite was thrown at a rival group. The attack was linked to the *CNN* gang. One official from the Victoria Sports Club said that a few months prior, a St Michael gang which was later identified as the *CNN* gang, shot holes in the clubhouse ceiling after a dispute broke out over a gambling game.

William (one of the members of the CNN)

William, who is now in his 50s, admitted that he used to be very vicious. Recalling an incident when he had gone to the Globe Cinema, he said he had encountered a man outside the cinema begging for $5.00. When he had responded to the man to "Carry ya ****!", the man told him, "Wait til you come out the theater, I will chop you up!" This threat had angered him, and he said that he had been unable to watch the movie with any level of comfort. His girlfriend told him "I know that man has you so offset."

He then went to Yabba (a gang member from *Jesus and the Disciples* gang) who happened to be in the cinema at the time, and told him he wanted a knife. Yabba had walked around the cinema asking for a knife and managed to get a knife for him. William had put it in his waist and at intermission, he had gone for popcorn. According to him, the man with whom he had the earlier encounter ran at him with a collins. The man slapped him in his back and "I went in his belly," William said. He had buckled and the guards and everyone then started running. The man's guts had started spilling out; the guards then turned and started pushing the man's insides back in.

According to William, the man is still alive today. He gave the man $1,000.00 and two big gold chains to dismiss the case.

His girlfriend who was the mother of his daughter, broke up with him after that and told him he "wasn't normal."

Kidnapped!

William said he travelled to Grenada, Venezuela and St Lucia and stole cocaine from suppliers and brought the contraband back to Barbados.

William recalled that there was a young man named 'Haitian', whose stepfather was his boss. Haitian was intelligent but William deemed him a trickster who believed he could talk his way out of everything. He would get the phone numbers of drug dealers, talk to them and then go down to the islands and meet up with them and trick them.

One on occasion, when he and Haitian travelled to Grenada, they were kidnapped by some henchmen on the island. What had transpired was that on a previous trip, they had stolen 2 kilos of cocaine from the Grenadians. On this return trip in question, the Grenadian men "snatched" them and took them into the dense Grenadian forest. They expected the worse. The Grenadians began interrogating the two men. However, they told them that although they had already transported one kilo to Barbados, they had hidden the other kilo at a secret location in Grenada and they assured the captors that they would get it the following morning.

In a story sounding like a movie script, Haitian and William were then tied up in a jungle and one man was left to guard them. Fortunately for them, the guard dropped asleep. William grasped the opportunity to untie himself. He then untied Haitian and both of them crept out from the area and got a taxi to the airport.

They had to avoid being discovered at the airport as they waited for their plane back to Barbados. While at the airport, they peeped through the airport louvres and noticed the 'Big Man' making drop-offs of other men who were departing the island to do business for him.

They eventually boarded the plane to Barbados without being detected.

William said that as the plane took off, and the land mass of Grenada was left behind, he told Haitian, "I am never returning to Grenada!"

War between CNN and Beirut Gangs

Many remembered when the *CNN* was at war with the *Beirut* gang which originated in the Marl Hole in Carrington Village, the City.

So bad was the situation that *CNN* made headline news, which is ironic as the news channel CNN was designed for that exact reason - to make news.

The murder of Rodney 'Sluggy' Howell on December 24th, 1990.

While there was always tension between the two groups, what caused the tension to spiral into a full-fledged war? Many persons were oblivious to what caused the war that escalated and erupted violently at Sheriff's Place on December 23, 1990 when a member of the *Beirut* gang was hospitalized. The following night, in a brutal reprisal attack, a *CNN* member, Rodney "Sluggy" Howell had his arm almost severed and received a fatal chop to the back of his head!

The residents from the community expressed fear because they said that they were hearing *CNN* members say that someone from *Beirut* had to die before Howell was buried!

This led to a series of events that transpired in School Gap and Prescod Bottom a few days later, where it was reported that one of the *CNN* members was on the prowl looking for a member of the *Beirut* gang. The war was escalating rapidly.

Recalling the incident that took his friend Sluggy's life, William confirmed there was an ongoing war between the *CNN* gang and the *Beirut* gang. Peter Rabbit from *CNN* and a man from *Beirut* were warring over a motorcycle. It was a situation where someone took the motorcycle and refused to return it. The friends from each side got involved and it morphed into a full-fledged gang war.

A month before Sluggy's death, William went into the Marlhole and took away the hat of a fellow called Dexter and told him *"Don't come round me!"* A series of events occurred after that.

William disclosed that a man from *Beirut* named Ed had shot him and he had chopped up Ed. William had chopped him up so badly, that Ed had had to be rushed to the hospital. William, too, had to be rushed to the hospital because he had been shot in his foot. He recalled that while in the triage, an orderly came up to him and told him that Ed was in the other room. He then rushed to go to finish him off, but was restrained by hospital personnel and was discharged forthwith from the hospital.

This started a war.

William and Sluggy would go in the Marlhole and shoot up everybody and "clear the Marlhole". He would go there on his BMX bicycle with a shot gun over his shoulders and "shoot up the place". They did not care about innocent persons being hit. In their opinion, if you were outside and in the environs of that community, you were guilty by association. "You can't be innocent, because you will carry back news."

According to William, sometime during the next few weeks, Sluggy decided he wanted to go in the dub (fete). At the time, Sluggy and William were living together. William was still nursing injuries from the shot in his foot.

"I pleaded with Sluggy to let my foot get better before he (Sluggy) went in the dub. Sluggy took up a big screwdriver and put it in his waist and went in Studio 10 in Fairchild Street, the City on Christmas Eve, 1990.

While in the club, two men who were members of the *Beirut* gang spotted him and a fight ensued and Sluggy was killed in the fight. According to media reports, the two men saw Sluggy outside Studio 10 and remembering what happened the month before, they decided to attack him. Media reports stated that Howell (Sluggy) was almost beheaded.

This led to retaliation and a full war between *Beirut* and *CNN* gang which included several drive-by shootings. William shot a man named Scums and was charged with attempted murder.

The *Weekend Investigator,* of January 4, 1991 reported that members of communities close to Tudor Bridge admitted that they felt terrorized by members of both the *CNN* and *Beirut* gangs.

Clash between CNN and Beirut in The Orleans

In that edition of the paper, persons from areas such as Hindsbury Road who were interviewed opined that the police force was not doing anything at all to alleviate the problems between the *CNN* and *Beirut* gangs. Some were of the belief that the police had taken a hands-off approach and were "waiting for them to kill out one another."

Another person from Prescod Bottom in Bank Hall told the media that the escalating violence in society should be taken seriously, as "all the members of both gangs are young and all are in possession of guns."

PETER RABBIT – AN INFAMOUS MEMBER OF THE CNN

Talking about his deceased friend Peter 'Peter Rabbit' Alleyne, William recalled Rabbit's great physical strength. "Rabbit was strong. Rabbit used to pull off or kick off the doors of drug pushers and body slam you because he was strong. He would come out on the block, make all the men on the block line up and tell everyone to give him a cuff in his belly. Who don't cuff him, Rabbit would beat them."

How Peter Rabbit died

According to one of the leaders, a Vincentian man brought some weed to Barbados. Rabbit and the men had the Vincentian man kidnapped in St George. On June 3rd, 1994, Rabbit and three other men - Matthew 'Kajoli' Wharton of Brittons Hill, St Michael, Fernando 'Swibbles' Graham of Mount Standfast, St James and Matthew 'Small Boy' Springer of Cemetery

Lane, St Peter - left Barbados with another Vincentian man on a boat owned by Peter Rabbit and Matthew Kajoli Wharton. They headed to St Vincent to get the Vincentian man's marijuana and were due to return that same night. They never returned.

'Peter Rabbit'

It was rumoured that the boat caught a hole and they tried to patch it in St Vincent. However, there were men in St Vincent who wanted them dead, so they could not stay too long in St Vincent, and had to push off the boat before it was completely fixed.

Another rumour had it that they were chopped up at sea and the boat burnt. Other reports suggested that the boat was blown up and the men killed, but this was never officially confirmed.

None of these rumours was ever substantiated.

However, in an interview with former members of the *CNN*, they confirmed that the men were heading home to bring up bales of marijuana; they surmised that the men were most likely killed at sea by persons unknown.

The drug trade in the 1980's and 1990's

One former CNN gang member explained that cocaine was very prevalent even back in the 1980's and 1990's. He does not think its influx can be stopped. He recalled that when the men would go to the Globe cinema for the 12:30 p.m. show to watch a Jet Li movie, inside would be filled with the scent of blackies (cocaine and marijuana mixed). He said while in the past they used to smoke blackies, the men nowadays are snorting.

Certain movies in the cinema and certain songs in the dub would make them hype. They would "buss a shot" in the air. He is convinced that the influence of music on the young people still continues. "Certain messages in the music clearly get people hyped. When you watch a karate movie and see all that kicking about, you leave the cinema and going through Bridgetown, we started kicking one another and garbage cans and anyone said anything to us, they would get kicked too," said William.

For certain crimes for which he was wanted, he had hidden for 3 years. He would not go in the dub or on the block. He bemoaned the fact that a lot of the youngsters nowadays cannot get this done. He said that he would hide at one of his girlfriends and would only come out in disguise wearing a wig. He said former detective Rap Brown had looked for him for

3 years for offloading two .38's in Black Rock. He remembered once when he had gone out, he had seen Rap Browne and had fled immediately.

How the CNN gang disbanded

The men said they had stopped the fighting and gang activity because they simply had grown "older and wiser." Their children also started to get older and they drifted away.

Some of the men started their own groups as well.

While William was at the height of a life of crime, he admitted that he had never been convicted of a crime. He had been remanded 16 times in prison, but had been able, like his counterpart in crime, to manoeuvre his way in the criminal justice system. He revealed that he had also spent two months in the Psychiatric Hospital for observation to see "if [he] was really mad".

"I never did time [in prison] because most of it was fighting and I paid out men who I chopped up; I took away dope men drugs, so I paid them out. I gave them big gold, gold chains, money, weed etc. I had their eyes dingling!" he boasted.

CNN's views on the difference between former and current gangs

One of the former leaders said that the difference between the gangs of yesteryear and now is the issue of respect. "I would now shoot at men and heading back home with a spliff and see my mother - I am outing that spliff fast! We had respect, but the youths of today have no respect for the elders." He believed too that it was because a lot of the parents were young.

He has also noticed the change in weaponry. "We used to move around with .32's, .38's and .357's. Now the men have more lethal weapons, like semi-automatics," he noted.

His concern also was that too many of the 'elders' still want to be involved in crime. "Give the youngsters their space. We had our time. Supply them and let them do their thing and be in the dark. Some of the old gangsters that still doing crime want to land their weed and be selling it themselves up front and the youngsters do not want that."

One of the other members also said that gangs today have different identities. They are all about controlling an area and a market. They are heavily focused on drugs and drug importation. Out of drugs, spiralled other crimes such as robberies.

"When police do a raid, and they seize a shipment, the men have to recoup the money that they lost especially if the drugs are on consignment. Suppliers must be paid. It is a lucrative business. If you do not pay, they will send their men or associates with a local gang to take you out, cos they want a collection," said one of the *CNN* men.

Yet another member lamented, "Nowadays the blocks do not live like in the past. Five and six men on the block and they don't live in harmony with one another. People on the blocks cursing one another, and that did not happen back then. That could not work for us as part of the *CNN*. We all lived in harmony."

One former member is currently developing a park in the area called RCG – Recognize Children's Growth. This is a park for the youth to develop themselves and is in an effort to change the stigma of the community where the name *CNN* has left a stain that still remains after all the years.

CHAPTER TEN

Jesus And The Disciples

Gang: We're just Disciples

Caption in Advocate newspaper Sept 29, 1989

Jesus and the Disciples, hailing from Shop Hill in St Thomas was a gang that was deemed to be problematic in the late 1980's. It comprised about 6 to 10 young men. One former member claimed that it was one of the most prominent gangs in Barbados at that time. Its leader was called 'Jesus'; the other members were his 'Disciples'. The leader is said to have suffered a mental breakdown.

Like the *CNN* gang, the Disciples engaged in violent disorders and terrorized persons in the north of the island. It was also involved in conflicts with other groups as well.

In September 1989, when a team from the Advocate newspaper visited the block where the Disciples were based, one of the members told reporter Geralyn Morris, "I don't have a job and I don't want one either." Ms Morris reported that this was the mindset of most of the gang.

The men of the Disciples at the time ranged from ages 15-26 and stated that they "just hang out together, fete together and defend one another," she had stated.

One of the members of the group said that he was expelled from school at 14 because he was a troublemaker and the teacher did not want him to be with his girl.

Another told her that his "old girl" gave him money every week in order to keep him out of trouble. However, he also told the reporter that if the occasion arose that he needed money desperately, he might do something that he would not normally do.

While the residents of Shop Hill did not see them as nuisances, this could not be said of many other communities.

Gang attack

Lee speaking to the media after his minibuses were vandalised by the gang.

On November 26, 1989, some men believed to be members of the Disciples damaged two minibuses, two houses and injured two people.

Morris Lee, the owner of the minibuses told the Advocate that he received a call around 12:30 a.m from residents of Hillaby, St Thomas, saying that two of his four minibuses had been damaged.

His driver was passing through Hillaby on his way home from a day's work, when a group of over 50 young men blocked the road, smashed the back window of the minibus, and would not let him continue his route.

The driver, who received injury to the right hand, was forced to abandon the bus and escaped to a nearby house, where he made the call to Mr Lee.

Lee told the media that one of the members of the gang followed his driver into the house and subsequently broke a number of its windows. The men then turned their attention to the conductor. He was robbed of the money-bag with the day's taking and had to flee to save his life.

It was not the first time that Mr Lee's vehicles were the targets of such lawlessness. Four months prior, one of his vehicles was attacked by a group of young men while it was traveling through Jackson and its back window was damaged.

Mr Lee, who was also the General Secretary of the Minibus Association, expressed grave concern at the time about the rise in crime and damage to other people's property involving the youth of the country. He also made a plea to those in authority over young people around the island.

In an interview with Trevor, a former member of Jesus and the Disciples, he revealed that he was a Christian and had been for the past 18 years. He sought to explain why he became involved in the gang.

The search for adventure and identity

He said that, unlike other gang members, he was raised in a structured and sheltered home where his single mother did everything humanly possible to maintain the appropriate structure and discipline. However, he wanted more – he wanted some kind of adventure. He believed that most men looked for this adventure in various places.

This search for adventure, he also saw, as a search for one's own identity and validation. While others looked to religion, relationships and other societal institutions, he found what he was searching for - an acceptance in the block and gang. This, he believed, is the reason why many young men join gangs.

He also remembered that his group developed a relationship with the men from the *CNN* gang – even though it was *CNN* and *Jesus and the Disciples*, in his opinion, they became one. He said that the lawless activity exploded after that unification: the fighting and the gang wars. He recalled that they were in a gang war with Melrose and then with men from Bush Hall.

The war that started in Melrose began when one of the gang members from *Jesus and the Disciples* got into an altercation with the men from Melrose and the *Disciples* wanted revenge. They beat up on a man from Melrose and they were arrested.

Sometimes, they would raid and take up the weed, dope, guns and whatever they could get their hands on. That was one of the ways they were able to get guns and drugs.

On August 11th, 1989 six members of the *Disciples* were involved in a disturbance outside a snackette in Belleplaine, St Andrew. They were remanded by then Magistrate Theodore Walcott.

In another incident, a young man of Church Street Gardens, Speightstown, St Peter, said he was attacked and robbed of his five gold chains by a member of a knife-wielding, weed-smoking gang from St. Thomas called "*Jesus and the Disciples.*"

Recalling the events which transpired at East Coast Road. St Andrew on Independence Day 1990, the young man told the court that while he was in the minibus B51, one 'Benn' held him by the shirt collar and "popped off" the chains which were valued at $1,600.00. Around 6:05 p.m. that day, he told the court, people had been boarding the bus, which was on its way to Speightstown.

He testified: "I actually saw the accused take the chains, and I saw one dangling in his hand. After that, he grabbed my shirt and said, 'You all want to test, you all want to test!'" This prompted him to get out and go behind the minibus where a youngster told him not to fight or get into anything.

Looking to be somebody

According to Trevor, many of the gang members come from single-parent homes and they are looking for acceptance. They are also looking for someone after whom they can model their behavior – something, he asserted, their fathers are supposed to be.

"They try to be Tupac, Michael Jordan, Biggie Smalls, they want to be somebody because they look on the television, see that individual, hoping that their dad can become something that they can model. When the dad is missing from the home, they look in various ways for someone to model what a dad or father should be. When you don't have that, anybody can become your dad, because you as a young man are looking for that person – 'I need my dad," said Trevor.

He continued: "If you look around Barbados, you will see – single parent, mother, two or three kids. Where is the dad? The dad is not around or he may be a dad that comes around, but how much influence is he going to have because a father living in a home with a mother and kids becomes the dominant force. He becomes that disciplinarian and whatever happens in there, they will be looking to that father.

"When that child reaches 15 years of age, and he realises that he is taller than the mother, how many women can restrain that young man?

"Now he is changing – his voice is changing, the people with whom he associates change and he comes to discover 'I am the man of the home'. So even though you may try to discipline me, I am taller than you and it is very challenging for that mother.

"Then you realise that key figure is missing… go in the jail and ask them who did you come up with? Most of them will say their mother, my grandmother, a sister, an auntie."

Even though he acknowledges that there are persons who grew up with both parents and still became deviant, he said that statistics should show that the majority grew up with a single parent.

Trevor admits that his mother did a very good job with him, and he was quick to say he has the best mother in the world. He said at the time, he did not accept her provision, her sacrifice and he went out and did what he did. However, his brother was the opposite of him – he was quiet and stayed indoors.

After he gave his life to the Lord, everything dramatically changed for him. Only then did he understand what parental care meant. "God has a tremendous impact upon you, because the Word of God teaches you how to become a parent – how to become a man and it shapes and moulds you whereby you can counsel people, because if you don't have that guide, it means that you will always spend your life searching... and a lot of them are still searching. What is it you are searching for? I don't know will be their response.

"Fame? Girls? Money? Even if you get those things, they will be limited and then how will they come? It will come through drugs, notoriety etc, so at the end of the day, what is it that you are lured by? You don't need the notoriety – it is always negative. You need something positive."

After his transformation came, Trevor went back to church which was significant for him because that is where the discipline came. He connected with Ministers who were able to help him. He went to deliverance ministries in the Caribbean, and there he connected with preachers and pastors. He went around Barbados ministering the gospel and that was what has been happening for him for a long period of time.

He said he was never shot, but shot at. "I was almost killed three times," he said. "I was shot at, bullets whizzed past me on at least two occasions."

He has been lucky - he was never convicted of the crime for which he was charged.

He disclosed that his gang was also in conflict with men from aynesville and the Ivy. Every week was a fight with some other gang member and he remembers a weekend when he went by one of his sons' mother. They had planned to go to Haynesville to a football match.

"I believe God was saying to me at that time, 'Don't go', he said. He followed the voice and stayed home. He later discovered that one of his gang members Corey, also known as "Yabba," had got chopped up at the match. He believed that if he had gone, he would have been chopped up as well.

A lot of the conflict was about gold, marijuana, guns, chains or snatching people's kangol hats. At the time, kangol hats were popular, and they would just snatch people's kangols in Bridgetown.

"Yabba, who is now deceased, fueled a lot of the robberies. He liked to rob people and come back on the block and talk about it," said Trevor. "For him, that was the most exciting thing. He liked putting himself out there and showing off about it."

Trevor recalled an incident when Yabba went to a family friend's house with two guns in his waist and lifted up his shirt, saying that he was 'hot,' but was just showing the guns and boasting.

The week before Yabba was killed in 2019, Trevor saw him at the bus stop and took him to Jackson where he went to connect with another notorious street person. Despite the fact that the *Disciples* gang had broken up years prior, Yabba still continued in the street life which inevitably took his life.

When asked why some of these men still continue with a life of crime even in their 50's, Trevor suggested that when one is a part of something for so long, because that is all one knows, one has a tendency to give everything to it.

"There are not a lot of individuals who came out that they can say that this guy came out and did something positive. If you look at most of these areas, depressed communities, you will continue seeing the same thing. Every day you are seeing people smoking dope, weed or fighting. **In order for you to be detoxed, you have to actually come out, but as long as you stay in it, you become a product of your environment.**

"Because those individuals do not have that leverage or that assistance to help them to get out, they stay in it. And when you stay in it, it becomes you. Sometimes, you don't want to leave it, because it makes you who you are, in terms of the notoriety, in terms of the money, in terms of the materialism – you are defined by that life."

Interestingly, members of the Shop Hill community believed that 'Yabba' was easy to lead astray. He and another man spent ten years in prison for robbing a minibus, but they only served about seven years. The other man came home, got a job and pulled himself away from a life of crime. However, that was not the case for Yabba.

He was arrested for possession of a gun at Spring Garden on Kadooment Day, 2014.

One resident said they saw Yabba the day he died, and he had received a call from someone and had rushed out the house to meet the person. He was later gunned down in Baxter's Road while in traffic.

Trevor believes for some men, the solution is God's divine intervention. He is active in the church and his presentation to the youth is about God. What he has been doing is trying to connect with some of them – those who have been in that life, and given their lives to God - to get them to testify. He is currently part of a male group where they sit down and talk about male issues. It is a fellowship for men who are struggling. He believes it really helps.

He also believes that there is no hope for many young people. Many of them are in the drug trade, because that is their way out. A fellow he knows said to him, "If you come up by me, you will see young girls. There is no hope. Mother and daughter in the house smoking weed, the girl goes outside, has sex to get money for her mother. There is no hope. There are a lot of those young girls who are on hard drugs, and the guys in the community are having sex with them for a few dollars or dope. It is bad. There is nobody giving you anything. There is nobody saying 'Come let me give you a job to elevate you.'"

He said this is very common in many of the depressed communities. "There is no one to elevate you." In order for you to be elevated, it has to come from within; where you go to school, you learn and when you come out, you do something for yourself.

"Even staying in there can have issues because there are people who will drag you down. I had to disconnect. Not that the guys are bad, but I HAD to disconnect!"

Brotherly love in the gang

One good thing he noted about his gang was the brotherly love and the camaraderie that existed among them. They were all devoted to the gang and they shared everything – not just weed, but money and some of them shared their homes. In his opinion, when one comes from a broken home, and needs somewhere to reside for a few days, other members open up their heart and their doors.

"You will find that kind of love. I believe that is why a lot of guys go on the block. You do not have that family conflict you find in your home. You have a brother in your house and he does not speak to you; you have two stoves in a house, two fridges in a house; your sister can't use your stove.

"A lot of those individuals leave those conditions and go to the block because, you see the block, you know you will not get that on the block, because when you get up there, the guys are going to cook and everyone will get something to eat."

One parting word of caution he had for those caught up in the gang lifestyle.

"When you come out of jail, you need an outlet such as an organization that counsels ex-gang members to come out of that life, because you are coming back to the same society. You need that positivity that can take you out of the norm – those things that you are accustomed to. If you do not have that outlet, you will be submerged into the same old ways and old habits that caused you to commit crime in the first place and take you back to jail.

"You need a structured after-care when you come out of prison. Right now, you do not have that."

He also believes that prison should be structured in such a way that hard offenders are not allowed to mix with offenders who commit minor crimes. He believes that when hardened offenders are allowed to mix with other offenders, it builds a network and when one comes out of jail, one will go and look for the other because "when things are not going well, I am going to come and look for you and you give me some dope or weed to sell... this becomes a recipe for disaster and you do not need that."

He said that all the men except Yabba are alive now and doing something meaningful with their lives. Most of them have their own businesses and have stayed out of a life of crime. Trevor said when he looks back, he concludes that it was just a phase they were going through.

And so is the case of *many* gang members – they grow out of crime.

CHAPTER ELEVEN

Scare Dem Crew/ Bird Gang

Before there was even a Scare Dem Crew, the block was referred to as **Hell Camp** in the 1980's and 1990's. It was alleged that people feared Black Rock men during those two decades. There were two brothers from Hell Camp who were feared. They would go out to venues like clubs and be shown nothing but respect.

The loose gathering eventually evolved, becoming more organised and was run by a man named Rick, who was a powerful boss. Over time, Rick and the men on the block had a misunderstanding, and for a long time, it was without a leader. According to one person from the block, the men did their own thing; so while the other gangs had relative order, Scare Dem had none.

Jerome "*Wild Geese*" Bovell, also known on the streets simply as "*Geese*" who was one of Rick's soldiers, stepped in to fill the leadership vacuum. Geese was feared. Even though he was just a regular member, he was feared, because "Geese was a gangster!"

Scare Dem, or the Bird Gang (as it was renamed in recent times), was located in Black Rock, St Michael and was a well-known block in the 1990's and early 2000's. This gang was often at war with other blocks and gained the attention of law enforcement for illegal activity. It was also a block that people feared.

Geese was the father of four children. He was a steel bender and a bar proprietor before being convicted for the use of a firearm and possession of ammunition.

One of the men interviewed from the CNN gang claimed that he 'brought out' *Geese* as a gangster. He said that when he and *Geese* had worked at Accra Hotel, he had loaned Geese a .38 to protect himself because he - *Geese* - and the men in Speightstown were at war.

At one point, Scare Dem crew and a group of Cave Hill men were feuding. Geese was shot in the stomach in the Eden Lodge area in 1998 and survived. When the media went to Scare Dem, Geese told them that men from a block called "The Cabin" in Cave Hill were responsible for the shootings occurring in Eden Lodge and Black Rock. He explained then that the bad blood originated between men from Cave Hill and Eden Lodge over drugs.

Geese said that as a result, police were constantly coming into the area and harassing the members of Scare Dem crew.

"People try to make Scare Dem look like a scary place but that is not so. Those are false allegations. Almost all the men are working or self-employed. We only come up here and lime on evenings or we play football. We are not involved in any war and want the violence to stop," Bovell (Geese) said at the time.

He admitted that there was animosity between men from the two communities which he claimed had been passed down from generation to generation.

"The men from Cave Hill just grudge us and we have nothing to do with them," he stressed at the time of the interview in 1998.

The wars between these communities, like other communities previously discussed, were over petty things like weed, women or some wars had even started from school days.

"A man may owe another man $10, but decides he is not paying it. It is not even about the $10, but it was about the disrespect!" said one man.

Geese at the time denied that Scare Dem was a gang and even claimed that the name "Scare Dem" was one that had been given to them by the Jamaican dancehall group of that same name.

"We are just normal people doing good things in this neighbourhood," he told the media.

However, Jerome Bovell would go on to make his own headlines one year later. He created a precedent by the changing the sentencing guidelines for firearm offences. This is the case as outlined in the precedent case which went to the Privy Council.

> Two policemen told the Court that on February 27 2000, they searched Jerome Bovell at a bar in Combermere Street, the City and found a firearm and ammunition on him.
>
> Nonetheless, Bovell's account of the events of that day was in direct contradiction to that of the police officers. He claimed that while he was in the bar in Combermere Street, five to seven police officers approached him, blocked the doorway of the shop and searched him in the presence of other patrons of the shop. All he had on him was Barbados money. After the

search, the officers took him outside and the officer in charge, one Brewster talked to him about a matter he was investigating. He said that they took him down to the Pondside and Brewster planted a gun in his right pocket while another officer put something in his back pocket.

Bovell said the officers radioed for others and eventually they took him to Central Police Station. At the station, he was interrogated about other matters and he was reported as saying that he told the officers that he had nothing to say unless his Attorney-at-Law, Mr. Randall Worrell, (now Justice Worrell), was present. Under cross-examination, he maintained that the pistol and ammunition were planted on him while he was walking between two officers without handcuffs. In effect, he was saying that, while walking with two officers, with his hands free, they put a loaded gun in his right front trouser pocket and ammunition in the back pocket of his trousers.

On July 28, 2000, the jury by a majority of 8:1 convicted Bovell on both counts and he was sentenced to 7 years' imprisonment on each count, the sentences to run concurrently.

The Appeal

Bovell filed 7 grounds of appeal but elected not to pursue the appeal against sentence.

According to the Appeal precedent, the guidelines in this case were designed to establish a sentencing pattern for firearm offences. The guidelines stated that in future, except in very special circumstances and for very compelling reasons, a custodial sentence should be imposed for offences committed contrary to Sections 3, 18, 19, 20 and 21 of the Firearms Act.

The Court of Appeal stated in its opinion that a person in possession of an illegal firearm is a potentially violent person and a potential menace to society.

Geese spent his time in prison and was released. However, he had several brushes with the law and would be incarcerated several times in his lifetime.

In March 2013, *Geese* was captured in Silver Hill housing area where he was hiding out after being placed on a wanted list by the police. He was incarcerated.

In an interview in prison in 2016, *Geese* said he finished school in 5th form and began smoking marijuana from around the age of 19. He also started selling marijuana from 23 years old and considered it to be very accessible once you knew who the suppliers were.

He considered himself at the time to be the boss/leader of Scare Dem. However, he considered his block to be a recreational place - an area in the neighbourhood where people came and limed. He said the block culture was just a community of persons liming and smoking but generations had now changed and so had the culture of the blocks.

"In my time, youngsters were not able to come on the blocks and lime or sell drugs. They could not disrespect elders either," he said. "Nowadays, the youth are very disrespectful to elders and are being accepted on the blocks."

Geese revealed that on his block, there was the drug boss (hustler) who would have to go to other blocks to get drugs if his block did not have a producer. He also disclosed that not everyone on his block was involved in selling drugs, only those who were not employed.

At the time, he said that guns and drugs were being imported together either through the seaport or legitimate traders. He said some men purchased guns legally and sold them on the streets at a higher price to make profits. Alluding to rampant corruption, *Geese* said he bought a gun from a retired official. When asked why he believed certain persons were involved in these criminal activities, his response was "money does talk".

He said that a way to prevent criminal activities from rising was to be stern with youngsters. He also believed that another way was to find some form of further skills training for the children now leaving school. He suggested that with regard to those unable to gain entry into the Barbados Community College, Skills Training and Samuel Jackman Prescod Polytechnic (now Samuel Jackman Prescod Institute of Technology), special programmes should be designed for them so that they would not be idle, which would result in them resorting to the blocks and ending up in trouble.

On one of the occasions when Geese was in jail, he conceptualized the idea of a Bird Gang. On his release, he brought home the concept of the Bird Gang to his community with some of his friends from prison. One member of Scare Dem said that men from Silver Hill and other places, whom Geese had met in prison, started coming on the block.

Then his mentor Rick was gunned down in a highly publicized murder. When Rick died, it changed Geese and he did not take it well. It was alleged that Geese called the block from prison crying.

Shortly after the interview, *Geese* was released from prison.

However, fate eventually caught up with Geese, and on June 28, 2017, he was gunned down near to his home in St Stephen's Hill, Black Rock, St Michael. He was just 44 years old.

One person noted that Geese was loved by the people in Black Rock. "He showed everyone love. You won't believe it was the same man." He also had a lot of influence.

Since Geese's death, the block had cooled down. "It was always a cool block," said one man. However, he said that many of the men joined either the 64 or Choppers, which are current gangs.

One of Geese's former soldiers, who admits to being a member of one of these current gangs, holds the deceased gang leader in high esteem. He said that the former gang leader was very different from the current gang leaders. According to him "Geese looked for his own things."

He said that Scare Dem, now called the Bird Gang never got along with the men from Chapman Lane, and it started when one of the men from the latter community snatched a gun from one of the Bird Gang members in a club. The man refused to return the gun.

Coming up as a little boy, he said that he always heard about Geese. "I liked him and wanted to be just like him." As a soldier for Geese, he said that Geese gave him anything he wanted. He gave him a bike to ride, a chain, weed to sell, and guns with which to protect himself and "to walk about with". He also said that Geese would send him into town to buy clothes for himself, which he found admirable.

"Geese will live on," said the former soldier who is now incarcerated. "When I go home from prison and 'breed' a young lady, my child will hear about Geese. Geese was a nice man," he said.

"I feel proud about Geese. Geese fought against the Queen in his case!" he said proudly. *N.B. It should be noted that this is a misconception on his part. He thought that Geese was actually suing the Queen, when in fact, he was suing the State.*

He said his only challenge with *Geese* is that he lived the life, but he had nothing to show for it. "If I live my life like this, at least I have to have something to show for it." He was adamant that this is what he wants to teach his children – to have something to show for this life if they so choose to live it.

CHAPTER TWELVE

Bloods And Crips

Bloods and Crips have their genesis in the USA and have been gangs for decades. Crips was started in 1969 in the United States by a 15-year-old schoolboy named Raymond Washington of Fremont High School, Los Angeles (LA) in the United States.

Bloods is a union of other gangs in the LA area such as the LA Brim and Piru Street Boys, in response to the massive membership base of the Crips.

In Barbados, a young man nicknamed O.B., a deportee, stated that he introduced Bloods into the island. The colours of Bloods is red: red and black beaded chains, red scarves; generally red clothing. Wearing black signifies leadership. Bloods flash hand signs in the shape of B's D's and W's.

Beads and flags - Bloods

Scarfs are extremely important to the identity of both Crips and Bloods. Both consider their scarves to be their flags. Bloods hang their flags from their right rear pocket. Crips hang their flags from their left rear pocket.

Rappers such as 50 Cents, the Game, Dipsets (Blood), Ja rule and Snoop Dog (Crips) are extremely popular amongst the youth.

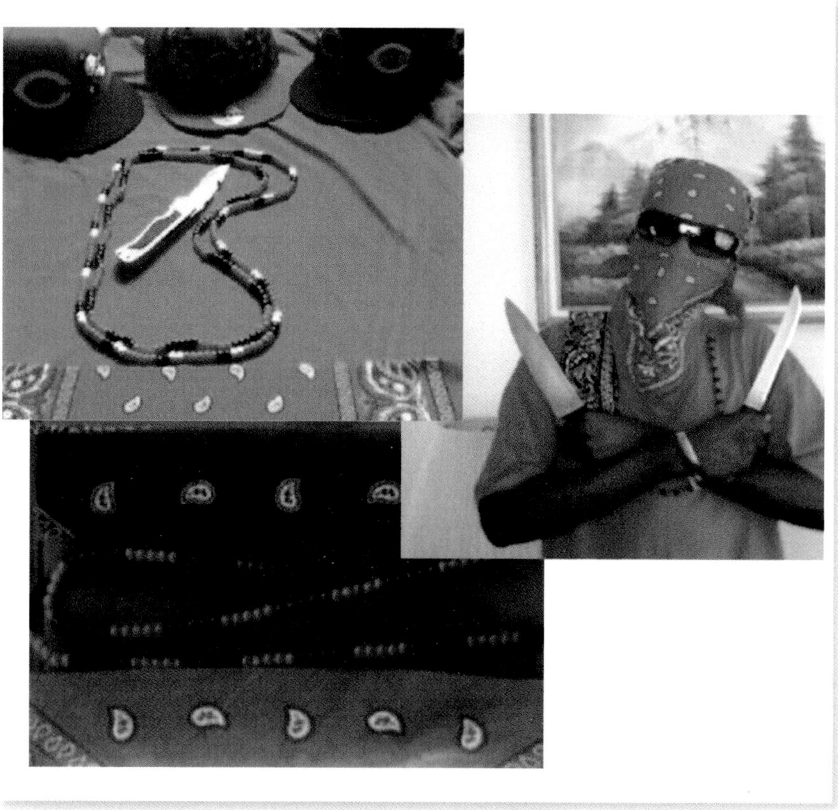

The above pictures were taken in Barbados

"100% DIRTY BLOOD MONEY I GET MINES THE FAST WAY SKEEMASK WAY!!!!!!!!"
The comment above by was made by the owner of this picture

Activities of Bloods and Crips

The two gangs like to display weapons and flash their respective group signs. These groups have no centralised leadership. Each set has its own hierarchy.

Blood gang tagging on a vehicle in Barbados in the early 2000s

CRIPS

"I used to live for the war" – former Crips gang member.

Crips wear blue. Blue and white or black beaded chains, blue scarves and blue clothing.

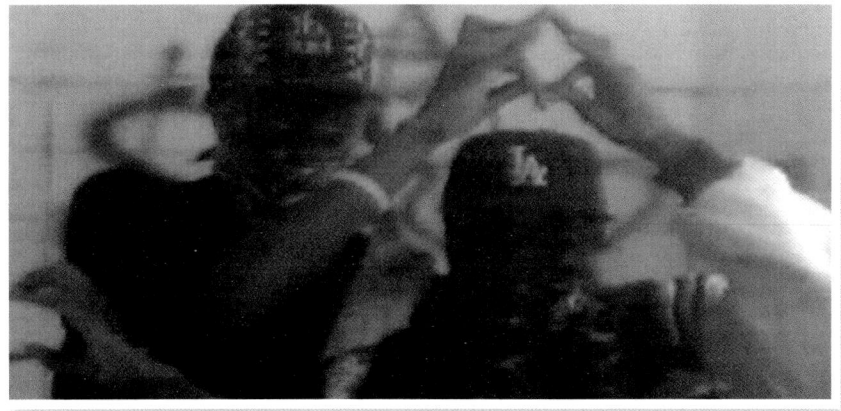

Crips flash hand signs in the shape of Cs and Ws

Crips tagging in a St Michael district in Barbados

INTERVIEW WITH FORMER CRIPS MEMBER

An extensive interview was conducted with Justin, a former member of the Crips gang in Barbados.

As a Crip gang member, one of the mottos was "You live for your mother, you live for your God, you die for your gang". Those at the top were the ones who basically lived for this motto.

According to him, many teenagers join the gang for the "badness" of it. He maintained that he had good intentions but the wrong approach. He claimed he could recognise the pain others endured and felt that he had to protect his people.

Justin was allocated to the Grantley Adams Secondary School. The first day at school, he saw someone's ear get chopped right off, and he thought "this school here cruel!" In his mind, he decided that it was "kill or be killed!"

One day he was on the basketball court and another student took away the basketball from him. He cuffed him in his face because in his mind - he didn't know if it was trauma from past lived experiences - but he would attack anything that he feared. From then, students and others with whom he came into contact had his back (supported him), and he had theirs.

The Principal complained that he was bringing gangs into his school. The group grew bigger and it then spilled into school wars – town versus country.

He came from Nelson Street, moved to the Pine at eight years old, and then on to Vauxhall at 12. At the time, his mother had recently married and was living in St Thomas. He was living in the country, but always felt connected to city life.

Justin was running his own little syndicate at the school. After school, he and his friends would take off their school shirts and wear black shirts with their school pants. They would go into town and war with the students from St Leonard's School.

They had orchestrated that they would "bore the bus" and throw "piss, shit and eggs!" The behaviour made the news. Even though he wasn't affiliated with the Crips from school, he said he always had the gang mindset.

A man named Red Rat, fresh out of prison, along with some other men, came to the school with a gun to kill him. At the time he was playing volleyball for the school. He had shown promise and his P.E. teacher had tried to mentor him. The men came with guns and he ran out to them with rocks. His teacher grabbed him to prevent him from going outside the school. The teacher took him to the office. He kicked the office door down because the Principal told him, "You won't stop bringing gangs in my school?" He was angry. He responded, "A man come to the school to kill me and that's what you are telling me?" He ran and tried to get back to the gate for the man.

By the time he got outside, the police had the man arrested and on the ground. The police also grabbed him and took him to the police station. He tried to scuffle with the man at the police station.

Justin said he was constantly getting into fights. It seemed that he was always either at the police station or the police would have to be bringing him home. His mother eventually pulled him out of school. He said he left school on a Friday and began working at a store in Bridgetown and that was when his interest in the Crips started.

"I would see these Bloods all the time and it was bothering me," he said. He started wondering where the Crips men were. He reached out to the underworld, joined the Crips and got his knowledge. He made sure his scarf was the longest. "You got to see me walking through town," he said.

"I started putting in my work. I started tagging and even went in the Red Zone tagging." Tagging is the use of graffiti to mark the name of a gang. He almost got killed in the Red Zone, a block in Marl Hole in the City. He went to a girl who lived near the block on a stolen bicycle. The bicycle was identified. He said he saw the men going in their stash and they started running behind him. He did not wait around! He took off and escaped.

He was an "O.G" (Old Gangster), a label affixed to a leader in the Crips. Some of the benefits of being an O.G. were getting money, protection and having soldiers.

Justin said he had the biggest numbers in terms of the Crips and he was the most aggressive O.G. While he had soldiers who would protect him, he preferred to be hands-on because he "loved warring". These wars included shootouts with rival gangs, robberies, beatings and chopping up other groups. It gave him an adrenaline rush. "When you finish a war, you sit down and talk with the boys ('You see when I had them running...') about all the things that happened in the war."

"Men in general love to be praised and honoured. It's just the nature of a man... any man. You tell a man 'You, you strong boy. Look how you holding dem bags!' and he has three bags. I guarantee you that the next day he has six bags holding. That's just a man.

"When you see a man in a particular path and getting praised for doing a particular thing, they will continue to do it. Like certain men that do murders and certain things and go back and do it again because they get praised for it.

"You can't just come and say 'I is O.G. now, I want my own gang! It doesn't work like that. You have to be accountable to someone. It is an organized gang with links.

"You must go through a G check, where you show them your knowledge, who brought you in the gang, certain oaths you had to recite and so on."

"The Crips and Bloods also had their special alphabet using signs with their hands. For example, B-K is 'Blood Killer'; I am on a blood kill so you throw out your set. The person is violating, so they are a blood killer or Crip killer. They were both blood killers and Crip killers in Barbados."

The former gang member recalled that a hit had been put on his head by the former head of the Bloods gang. He was walking through the minibus stand when an elder from another gang encountered him and told him of the hit. He thought that the elder was the person who had been assigned to do the hit and said to himself "Well you know what you have to do."

In his head, he was telling himself, "I know I won't be here long so when I go down, I going down in glory!"

However, the hit on his head never materialized.

Pressure from law enforcement

Law enforcement started to pick up on the Bloods and Crips. Police began to crack down on, and learn more about these groups; the different colours associated with them; what these colours represented; and the identity of the gang members.

In addition, according to him, there were policemen who were affiliated and who would put them on their guard. "They were not deep and banging, but they would associate using "cuz" or "loc", (pronounced "look). The police would contact them and tell them to "keep it low", that their name was "ringing" in this particular area or that someone was trying to figure out where a member of the gang lived exactly.

He was young (early 20's) when he became an OG, which was rare. OG's generally were not young. They were more mature and "had to put in work" to become an OG. However, he had made up in his mind that this was the life he wanted to live and he did not have much fear. He also had made up his mind that if he did indeed have fear, he would attack that fear to overcome it.

Recruitment:

The Crips recruited members from every secondary school in Barbados. These recruits were referred to as "set members."

The members of the Crips had a 'loc' which was their Crip name. Instead of calling them a Crip, they were called a 'loc'. Those were the names for Crip members. Everyone had aliases, but this ex-gang member said he did not want an alias. He wanted his name known.

He admitted that it was scary because he would tag the walls and use his name and not an alias.

Group of young Barbadians displaying the Crips colours and signs (early 2000s)

Near death experience

In 2010, he had just finished recruiting new gang members and was walking through Bridgetown. Admitting that he was young and inexperienced, Justin got himself in a situation where a man from Haynesville approached him in Roebuck Street and asked him ,"Wait. You is Justin? You supposed to be de bad man?"

"Wait. This man is a freak or wuh?" Justin said he thought to himself. "You questioning me... and it's how he did it, with no respect! Justin pulled out his scissors and the other man ran into a store where they started fighting. Justin's scissors dropped and he head-locked the man, while he was scrambling for the scissors. The man retrieved the scissors and started stabbing Justin. He got stabbed in his shoulders twice, his spine and the back of his neck. The blood started splattering on the walls and people in the store started to scamper. He then passed out, but was later revived.

Police arrived on the scene and he told them that the man had tried to snatch his chain and he was defending himself. He was hospitalized. While in hospital, his mother tried talking to him and told him, "You have to come out of this life."

But according to him, the incident only made his popularity grow by leaps and bounds. On the streets, the word was that Justin had been stabbed five times...and survived!

While in the hospital, a nurse asked him, "Who are you?" He asked her why. She told him "Look through the window."

When he looked through the window, he was amazed. The gang members were all in the car park throwing up their hand signs. He did not know he had so much love – the Crips love. According to him, "That put a battery in my back."

Other gang members assured him that they would retaliate on his behalf. When his mother came to visit him, she warned him. "You have to make up your mind. You have to live for these men or you want to live for good." He responded, telling her "But these are my family too."

From that time, his name was "ringing" which gave him 'street creds' and he got more recruits. According to him, he became bigger than ever. "It was like 50 Cent being shot and his reputation went up!"

He left the hospital, even before he was fully healed and went into town with his bandages on his body. He could not wait to get back on the streets. "While walking through town, my numbers were crazy... just crazy, crazy, crazy," he said proudly.

His gang members were looking for the man that stabbed him but couldn't find him. Then one day, he received a call that the man they were looking for was in Sheraton Mall. He said "Sheraton? This man gotta be mad!!!" Sheraton was his base for the Crips.

By this time, his gang had unified gang members from both Vauxhall and Sheraton areas. It was not just Vauxhall men, who were originally the Electric City men, and had become Crips. The Sargeant Village men, who had once been his rivals, had joined a gang called Blue Street and were also aligned with him. They were more into robbing people and though he wasn't interested in that part, he figured if he got them to link up with him, he would be "bigger than ever."

He said that the Sargeant's men were like hyenas. "You cannot tame them, just let them do what they want to do. They would shoot at one another. The people in Sargeant's were like monsters. Because I knew this, I knew how to work with them and I knew that they feared me too."

He also knew that they had guns, so he went into Sargeant's Village and told the men "Yea, the man up here." Carrying a gun, he went up by the Olympus cinemas intending to have a shoot-out with his attacker. "I said that this man will hold some shots today!" However, it was a Saturday and children and crowds of people were in the mall; security was everywhere; cameras were everywhere.

The man saw him and it was a standoff.

Justin told himself that if they followed through with the hostilities there at the mall, they would all get locked up.

The men who were with him started getting cold feet, which angered him. Nothing happened and he ended up walking away.

He went home, and straight-away went to what was then MSN on his phone and posted on his status "I done with the Crips. I is a street soldier." According to him, the YSGC (a rival gang) and other rivals and other OGs started to be intimidated by him. Plus he knew other Bloods that wanted to move with him. In his mind, he did not have it to be a gang thing.

People started contacting him and asking him what was a 'street soldier' and telling him that they wanted to join him. The word spread quickly about him being a street soldier. He created his own group, recruiting both Bloods and Crips. The colours were army green. He also made an alliance with another group called The Last Resort Family whose colour was orange.

He continued to 'put in the work'. Street soldiers was born. Their signs were two S's.

Street Soldiers

After he formed the group, the hit increased on his head. For obvious reasons, neither the Bloods nor the Crips liked that he was carrying away its numbers.

"At the end of the day, people knew I loved the war. I used to live for it. I used to go at your house and wait at ya front door. I had made up my mind I was going to die like this. There was nothing to fear, but I know how I going out and I going out blazing!"

Justin said he felt invincible. He would go to rival gang members' houses and sit down and wait sending a psychological message that this man is not afraid of them.

Due to his connections to the boss from Electric City, he had a lot of backing from that group as well. People liked his spirit, he claimed.

Street soldiers was prominent for a long time until the police started cracking down on the gang. He had enemies, but still had a lot of respect. There were hits on his head, because he had disrespected the order, but everyone who came in from overseas to do the hit actually told him that they had come to kill him but surprisingly showed him a lot of respect and told him to watch his back. The threats were real – not only against him, but also against his sister and mother. He was prepared for a violent death and told himself that it would happen. He believed it to be inevitable. It had stressed and depressed him, but he knew that he was in too deep to ever get out... alive! The only way out was death.

What changed the game?

Ironically, Justin played in the movie *Hush* as a gangster. He was chosen because he was well-known and he was a dancer on the streets at the time. However, they did not know his deep involvement in gang life.

Those who idolized him and saw him in the movie cheered him on because, as he put it, "in their head, they seeing me playing me" in the movie.

The producers, who did not know that he actually did live a gangster's life, asked him to talk to children about avoiding the life of a gangster! What really touched him and changed his mindset about gangster life was when the producers asked him to speak to students at the Challenor School. The Challenor School is a school for children who have special needs. Some of the students asked "You is Justin?" and started to display their scarves, telling him, "I want to be just like you." These vulnerable children, totally oblivious to the hits that were on his head, saw him as a role model. The movie's producer noticed it too. "Do you see the influence you have on these children?" It all affected him greatly.

At the time, the constant talk on the streets about shooting and killing his mother and sister had him depressed. He was preoccupied with the pressure from the police and the strong premonition that he would soon be killed.

"Every day, I would listen to this particular song, because in my mind I know I gine dead. Every day I left home, I felt death over me. I would say 'Today might be the day!'"

The gang started to disintegrate. People started going to prison. Some of the men in his gang started to betray him and he could not trust them anymore. Some men from Sargeant's Village came home from prison and conspired against him, trying to create their own set, even though they did not have the knowledge. This hurt him. He had had enough.

He said to himself, "If I dead, I dead but this is what it is." He also started talking to God. "God if you real, come through."

He started telling others he was done with the gang-life, and some persons started to follow him in the same pursuit. The word started to spread.

One day, he was walking alone through Queen's Park near to the Central Bank. This was not a usual practice as he was always with someone.

Suddenly, about 20 Blood gang members saw him and their eyes "lit up like hyenas!" He remembered saying to himself, "This is it boy, don't run. Don't fight back. Just walk on the other side of the road." He said, "God, if this thing real and you real fuh trute, you got to come through for me." He was determined that he was not running or fighting, and he went on the other side of the road.

They started pulling out weapons. He said again to himself that the day was coming and he was mentally prepared for it.

At the same time, a car pulled up, hit brakes and the driver told him, "Get in!" He got in the back seat. The man did not say a word. As the Blood men surrounded the car and the man scratched off.

The man took him straight to the makers of the movie who were at Praise Academy at the time. The man put him off and left. To this day, he does not know who the man was. He stood up in the middle of the road with a bewildered look on his face. He then went upstairs the Academy where a session was taking place.

There was a man who was a deportee telling his stories about the drug boss in the States and how he had changed his life.

He came over, tapped Justin on his shoulder and told him "Don't worry. You will get through it."

"This man know who is me? I was so confused". But he was convinced. "This God thing has to be real."

After that, he started behaving differently. People, including other gang members, started coming up to him and saying to him, "I hear you change" and gave him respect. He was very confused.

According to him, a lot of the gang started dissolving and started to fall (evolve) into geographical gangs.

He was surprised. He had not expected it to deteriorate so quickly. He insisted that Crips are still around but in other gang forms. A lot of the gangs have also gone into the more established gangs.

"One will see the Choppers putting up the C's. Instead of calling themselves Crips, they will just call themselves where their geographical base is at the moment," Justin explained.

He said if he goes to certain places, he will still get respect from certain people. Some will still give you a handshake. The younger ones, however, who have now come on the scene, do not know the history.

When he made the change, he "backslid a little" and went to a fete where a man came up to him, and said aggressively, "You is Justin?"

That move triggered him because he did not like people asking him those sort of questions. That old suspicious gangster was still inside of him. He was going to counter with, "Boy, move from in front me!" However, an inner voice commanded him to humble himself.

He replied to the man, "Yeah, man."

The man asked him "Yeah, you outta that gang life? I hear you change and thing, yuh know."

"Yeah, man. It's true," Justin told him.

The man looked down and Justin followed his glance to a gun in the man's waist. The man told him, "If you had said anything else, I woulda shoot you right here in you stomach and burn you for sure, right now. I respect that you change. I would love to get out of this life but I can't get out. I in too deep."

As fate would have it, the same man ended up committing murder. He was beaten on a pasture and went to prison. He was a Blood but he tried to transition. He was killed in prison, according to Justin.

When asked about what had happened to many of the other gang members, he said many of them were killed, police scared them, many were no longer powerful and also circumstances change and people change with them. A lot of them don't have what it takes to live that life anymore. A lot of bosses just want to be bosses – they are not active.

"Everything nowadays is centred around money. Some well-known bosses gave the men bikes. They put money in their pockets, give them cars and tell them 'Keep that'. The worst thing you can do is give a poor man something. He will always feel indebted to you. The boss doesn't associate with them in terms of going out; it is strictly on a business front.

"The amount of heights and gated communities that the gangsters live in is also a stark difference. It is more sophisticated. You are seeing gangsters in places that are usually reserved for the upper class. They do not look like the typical gangster. You do not see them in ghettos, but if they do, they pass through, come and collect and move off.

"Others are doing legitimate businesses such as landscaping businesses to clean their money."

Justin stressed that social media has also changed a lot of things in the gang world. Back in the 1990's and early 2000's, there was no social media. He said it is also causing a lot of gangsters to get arrested.

"The ones at the top rarely get touched, and when they do get touched, there is the "fall man" who will go to jail for the gangster. This is commonplace in the gang or even street culture." Justin himself admitted that he was willing to go to jail for a friend of his who was facing a gun and ammunition charge. They surmised that if his friend went to jail, he would be sentenced for a long time, but since Justin had no convictions, he would only get a fine.

He said he was willing to take it because of the love he had for his friend; he did not want to see him go to jail for a "slip up". He said the friend had not wanted him to go through a conviction for him since he had changed his life. However, the friend did eventually get a fine for the gun and ammunition possession conviction.

He also noted that women are still actively bringing drugs into the island and are willing to take the risk because they are of the opinion that no one is being incarcerated for drugs anymore, especially if they have the money.

"The fella on the block probably will do a little time," he stressed, "but once you have the right connections you will be covered."

In his opinion that is one of the things that has changed from his time as a gangster. "In my time, we were not even warring over drugs. It was over historical beefs. Now, it is more interlinked because of money. The majority of the men, especially from town have the same boss on a different level, so the boss has to out a lot of the flames by talking to the men about the warring as "it is not good for business". You can't control the ones that are affiliated but still not affiliated.

"Rather than have war, they try to get rid of the war factor. The war thing is for the underlings – the young boys mostly. At the upper level, all the gangsters talk.

"If I had to go back in the game, I am not going back as the same Justin. I will still be working, driving a proper car, not surrounded by no gangs or no blocks or nothing so. I know certain people now. I know how to operate with certain things. I won't have to get my hands dirty and if I had to get myself in beef, you can give a fella $2,000.00 and tell the fella 'I want he hit for me.'"

Regarding the issue of a hitman, Justin disclosed that "Once you give a youngster who has nothing - give somebody something that don't have anything - they will be loyal to you. Picture this here – a man now come out of school. His mother put he out; he has nowhere to live. He there by a girl today; he friend tomorrow. A man come to him and say 'Hold this in you pocket. Tek care of yourself. I got you – you is my brother.' Next day he sees him and tell him, "Buy a food for yourself. Let we go in town and buy some clothes. I buy clothes for myself and some for him. You believe if I ask this man to do anything for me, he gine tell me no? He ain't gine tell me no because I am the only man that ever show him love.

"So when I tell you, 'Hear this. I got a situation here though.' I put a weapon in his hand and tell him, 'I want this handle', he gine do it, because nobody never really care about him that sorta way and that's what happens to the majority of these youngsters.

"I tell you – give somebody a pair of shoes that never had shoes. That means way more to them than anything else."

He left this daunting message. "The work to reform these men will be very difficult. It is hard for me to tell somebody that brek to change their lives. Hard".

When he was younger, he admitted that he was shy and timid. His cousin, who was eventually murdered, told him, "You gotta stop with this shy thing." He carried him on big blocks at the time with a shot gun in his hand or a baseball bat sometimes and basically shaped some of his behaviour. He would cry and tell his cousin, "Man, mummy ain't love me." His cousin told him, "When I was your age, I was in Dodds. I promise you, as long as you live, you would never go through the things I went through and you got to stop crying. This crying thing ain't gine change the situation." This hardened his heart. That's how his cousin dealt with it, because he too had had nobody for him.

Just before his cousin was murdered, he was trying to change his life. He went and took passport pictures with the intention of going to St Vincent to start a new life. He said his cousin would have had to have known death was coming. "You could feel it." But it was too late. He was murdered before he got the opportunity to migrate.

His father never was home and "didn't even check to see if his clothes were pressed". He would go days and days without seeing him. He had no electricity and he had to go to the standpipe to get water. He was just living in town, surrounded by killers, thieves and robbers. He said he remembers going to church people and asking for money just for something to eat or for bus fare and they would just walk past him.

He recalls how he would go in the Fountain in Independence Square where people would flip coins and dollars and he would go in the Fountain and collect money to buy at least some sweet biscuits.

He became resentful. He felt abandoned, and believed that no one cared about him. Justin remembers encountering a school boy who told him "Wait, how you feel I does get my school things? I does got to rob people."

The boy boasted about how he made $2,000.00 just pulling off robberies.

Justin said to him "Fuh trute? I gine come and chill with you tomorrow night!"

Justin stated, "You hungry, you stomach growling yuh know and nobody ain't care nothing about you. So eventually you have that mindset, I can't care bout nobody no more then.

"Then you carry that mindset... you know what I gotta do? I will start robbing people; rob prostitutes and at least I getting something to eat and then I can go back to school."

According to Justin, he wanted to go back to school and to live with his mother in the country. One day, he rode up to his mother's home on a bicycle that he had stolen from a city area and when he arrived at his mother's residence, he saw his mother, her husband and his brother sitting at the table eating. He said that destroyed him! He just rode past the house without stopping and rode back to Bridgetown. He said that night, his head was on fire! He committed a lot of crime that night.

His mother eventually came back for him and told him to come back home. All his school books were bought by then. But it was too late. He had, in his own words, "already turned into a monster".

When asked about teachers whom he looked up to and who could possibly have steered him away from the path he was on, he answered saying that he thought most teachers were just there to collect a salary and go about their business. Plus, he pointed out, there were too many children to police, agreeing that the teachers could not 'mother' all of them.

One teacher however stood out – his physical education teacher, who he said had genuine love for him and tried to get him involved in sports, but the influence of his environment was too strong.

On a happy ending, his former principal who chastised him for bringing gangs to his school, invited him back to the school to give a speech to the current students. He was presented with an award recognizing him as an outstanding past student and he really did appreciate that gesture.

He is now involved in a charity where members would talk about situations plaguing young people and about programmes to create solutions. They also go into schools and give back to the school children, but funding was limited, so he has tried to raise his own funds. His charity recently conducted a virtual legal clinic and a job rally. So, Justin is a success story, and for that, we wish him the best!

CHAPTER THIRTEEN

Chapman Lane And The Orleans

On the outskirts of Bridgetown lie two neighbouring inner city communities: New Orleans, better known as The Orleans and Chapman Lane.

The Orleans is laid out as ten avenues that run parallel to each other and is a relatively large, densely populated community. The parallel layout of the avenues in The Orleans seems orderly, despite the narrow streets.

Chapman Lane is equally dense in terms of residents, but by contrast, the street layout is somewhat less orderly. Severe dislocation of the residents was imposed in the late 1970's and early 1980's to create room for the Bridgetown Sewage Plant. This community still bears the scars of progress from those years.

Chapman Lane is considered a community that looks out for its residents. "Chapman Lane would cushion you. It was about unity. All types of persons lived in Chapman Lane. It was an energy," said one former resident. It is considered not only one of the most together communities in St Michael, but a defensive community that honours its own.

Neighbouring rivalry

According to one resident of Chapman Lane, the disagreements between Chapman Lane and The Orleans started many decades ago as a rivalry in sports such as basketball and football. They believe it was a matter of envy and jealousy. People who succeeded in life such as in sports became the envy of others. Wars also came about through gambling.

Cuthbert from Chapman Lane, Dolphus and Big Mike from the Orleans were considered one man armies back in the 1970's. "They didn't have any teams. They would come and beat you with their bare hands. When the men started going out together, they would fight."

The residents said jealousy is what caused the war between groups. Earlier it was sports, but other factors had since come into play. "Now it is transactions that went bad, a man went to do 'business' with another man and one of the men 'locked' his things and kept his money - that increased the violence."

But another resident said that the separation came about due to the grandchildren of that earlier generation. "Before the war, Chapman and Orleans were one people," said one resident. "We would breed into one another and everyone lived well with each other."

Some had other views on what caused the division. "There were specific elements within Barbadian society that have divided these two communities," was the opinion of a number of residents. They stressed that these elements were dividing and ruling. They claimed that these people felt they can do anything better than black Barbadians. The black Barbadians were bringing the drugs and these groups decided that they too would bring in drugs. However, it is more likely that this involvement is the result of the realization of the profits that could be generated by trafficking in drugs.

"The difference is that these minorities have the money and resources to do it, so they are now controlling the gangs in the area. They have the blacks killing each other," opined another resident.

"Essentially, they are doing the same thing that was done to us in slavery where persons were converted into Christianity. The young people are not seeing it and they are being brainwashed, but you cannot tell these young people anything," complained one resident. These are the grandchildren to whom the resident referred; citing their lack of community spirit and a working knowledge of the history of the area.

In an interview with a resident from New Orleans, they recalled that when money flowed, a lot of drugs came from Chapman Lane. The drug trade was started in a gap in Chapman Lane. There were small elements selling marijuana and this led to many police raids in the community. Then, according to this resident, "came the monster – cocaine rocks.

"A young man from the Orleans started bringing cocaine powder in the mid-1980s. This young man had other young men from surrounding areas who helped him. His nephew made it a business by keeping his books for him.

"Fatman started selling cocaine as well as marijuana. I saw Annie, Sue, Joan and Violet all get hooked on rock. They prostituted themselves to get a hit. Then other men in the community started selling it too.

"Men would steal gold, break into places in Fontabelle, steal from construction sites and sell their stolen property for $5, $10 to support the habit," he said.

A few of the women managed to get out of the habit and led normal lives afterwards. However, he recalled that it destroyed Annie while some women contracted AIDS trying to support the habit.

The Orleans resident recalled that the area once had boundaries of what they would and would not do, even as it related to stealing. However, a young man moved into 6th Avenue and brought a new set of technology into Orleans. He taught the fellows new techniques to breaking and entering, and according to him, business people started cementing their roofs. New Orleans began to be stigmatized because of these new criminal elements.

"That is why it is important to watch who comes into your neighbourhood," said the resident.

Thug Life

New Orleans had a crew/gang called *"Thug Life"* in the 1980's. Interviews were conducted with some of its former members.

One of the interviewed elders from Thug Life stated that he was the leader and had his soldiers under him in a defined hierarchal structure. He also was a form of community leader. When children's parents could not afford to send them to school, he would give them lunch money. This earned him a lot of respect on the street for the type of elder he was.

According to him, members of Thug Life were "good men." They would hustle as carpenters, masons and other trades, but when they were home and came together, they would go and party. If someone disrespected one of the men, "a fight would brek from there". The men would arm themselves with collins (machetes) and knives among other things, but not with guns in those times. "There were no guns those times...chop ups with knives and collins for ya," he said.

At present, there is the Young Thugs where the age range is from 17 to manhood, and the Old Thugs, which are the original Thugs.

Respect on the streets

The all-important concept of respect and not ever allowing oneself to be disrespected is a recurring theme in this book. The Thug Life was no different.

"A man in the club mash your brand name shoes, or you see a man wukking up pun you girl and you gone in the club with you crew and you know where you from... all of we from the Orleans. Everybody gine step and the opposing side from say, St George will step and it will become a war and it will start an enemy vibe from there," said one woman who limed in the area.

"Sometimes they even forget what the fuck they fighting over!" The youths come along and don't even know what the war was about but they get caught up in it."

Thug Life has evolved with the advent of guns and drugs coming in from neighbouring islands, and the USA. The men on the street gravitated to a particular person who became the boss "because the boss, who is not from the community - had the connections and "could make things happen". According to the elders, the young Thug Life that currently exists is divided with one person not speaking to the other. One elder lamented that when his money went, some of the younger generation that came up under him took over. The older Thug life members acquired jobs, cars and started families. In his opinion, having children made a lot of the older Thug Life members get out of the game.

Some men moved out to other gangs and hopped from one block to another. According to the former Thug Life members, a 'block hopper' is very dangerous. They bring information back to the enemy and reveal the structure of the block, its connections, where the weed and guns are stashed ... a lot of these things start wars.

The elder who was interviewed was landing drugs from St Vincent and was able to make those drug connections with other neighbouring territories, whilst hustling drugs on the streets. "Life was good back then," he said. Money was flowing and women were flowing and even fighting over him.

He chose to get out after the guns started coming into the country more frequently.

One of the key drivers for his getting out of the game was his children. He had been shot already; his house had even been shot up because of a feud. Some young boys from his area went into town and caused a scene with another gang. The gang men felt disrespected, so they retaliated and committed a drive-by shooting in the community and his house came under fire.

According to the former Thug Life members, the gang men were humble back in the day. "The generation of gangsters are different now. They will start a war anywhere, anyhow, with whoever is there. It has escalated to mothers getting shot for the actions of their sons.

"The young men ain't tekking no lot of talk. If you tell a man you gine shoot he, mek sure you got your gun on the spot because you will be shot."

"About three weeks ago, a man came to me and told me he wanted wrappers and a fanta. He just walked up the road and was fatally shot."

Gangsters would come and tell him, "Listen I don't want to shoot up your place, but I got somebody to shoot out by you," and they would carry out the threat. He witnessed three men get murdered in his gap because of gang violence.

One of the women, who is the girlfriend of the elder, witnessed her son-in-law murdered before her eyes two months prior. He was begging for his life, and she saw when they shot him. She did not hesitate and rushed outside to his aid. She believed that he died because of association and because the young people do not have any education.

Her own son was also murdered 6 years before that. The couple has a son who is in hiding. The son, who is also in the game, went to prison, came out and as soon as he came out, two masked men came and shot him. He had to move from the area for fear of his life.

Another member of the group stated that some of the police are involved in the game. "When police hear you got big things, they come for you and tax you."

What is causing the wars?

The responses were interesting.

"If I land 200 pounds of weed now, I selling my weed, making money and I buy a car and put two gold chains around my neck …the red eye man out there saying you have too much so he will rob you."

"We conditioned to look good and show off, not to invest."

"Don't get tie up. They have police in gangs too. They take the weed they hold from people and give a man to sell for him."

"When nothing happening for you and people hungry.… that police salary of $2800.00 is not going a long way and they have mortgage and car loans to pay and still wife and children to take care of….that slave pay ain't saying nothing…and that same police hearing that a man out there selling 1,000 pounds of weed.…"

"Some of these men who are warring with each other went to school together, but as they got older, they picked up old wars too, generational wars that they didn't know anything about; and then they increased the war. Some of the men fathers or brothers were murdered and they carried on that same war, not knowing what going on but listening to hearsay on the streets. So listening to wrong information and getting caught up and bringing enemies against one another as well.

"Another factor that brings war is association – you associate with the wrong person – someone they do not like, they want to kill you."

As members shared their stories, they talked about how violence came to their own home. A former female member of Thug Life stoically talked about how the father of her grandchildren was murdered just outside the window of the home where the interview was taking place. She said emphatically that "while they could not tell me why he was murdered, they believed it was because of association."

They also believed that music played a role in shaping the behaviour of the men in these communities. "Movado and Kartel played a role in some of the gang-related incidents that happened here," one lady surmised. "Some of the young boys picked up the Jenna, Gully and Gaza thing, the red and blue (Bloods and Crips) and it affected young impressionable men and women locally and regionally.

"Wars started over a lot of talk, this person don't like this person, some people picking up fire rage, over girls…people watching other people's success."

One middle-aged man who used to live in the area, but has since moved out, said that in his time people were looking for money through drugs, and there were no wars. People were intimidated because he was from Chapman Lane. Chapman Lane had a lot of bad boys in the 1970's and 1980's.

He recalled that in 1986, he had access to a gun. He bought a gun for $50.00, a .25 automatic. He had no reason to buy it, he and no one were in a war, but he had the money to buy it and a man approached him and sold it to him. One day, he took the gun to Barbados Community College and it dropped and shot the toilet. He panicked because in his view, he could have accidentally shot someone. He took that opportunity to give it away and never owned one again.

He believed that this generation is the generation of vipers and society has changed for the worse. He is also of the opinion that the influence of American rap culture has a major role to play. Lack of parental guidance plays a role. When he was growing up, he had to be inside by a certain time. He bemoaned the fact that nowadays at 10 - 11 pm, one can see little children roaming the streets. He fondly recalled that when he was a child, he could never be on the road at that time. "When 7:30 p.m. came, I had to be in bed. That was the rule."

He related how he once overheard a youngster asking an older man for $5.00. The man took it out and gave him and then turned around and told the youngster to whom he had given the money, "I hope when I ready to put a gun in your hand and you have to do 'work', I hope you do 'work', you know." He was appalled and he said to him, "This is the sort of mentality you are pushing towards this boy? You wouldn't encourage him to look for a job, stop in school, get an education, nothing so?"

It disturbed him.

> *"Drugs feed the community. You can't take drugs out the community. Wars are seldom about drugs." –*
> *New Orleans resident*

In an interview with a young man from the Orleans, he said he got involved in a life of crime from around the age of nine, because it was the life to which he had been exposed. From around the year 1996 when he was about 15, he would beat up people because he grew up seeing people successfully do it to other people. He would rob them and take away their gold. He said that he grew up around Thug Life in the Orleans and this was what he saw and learnt. According to him, in the 1990s, everything in the Orleans was Thug Life. There were only two gangs in the Orleans back then - Thug Life and Gambino.

"We used to beat people and tek way their things, but we didn't really used to harm nobody," he stressed oblivious to the contradiction. "There would be licks, but not like how today is. Today the youth would come to tek your things and they would shoot you."

When asked why they would beat and rob people, he said "The truth is now that I get older, we did not know nothing much.

"You were going to school and learning things and coming home and seeing other things and you were like 'Yea, you gotta get money, you gotta buy shoes'. Mumma don't have no money to support you, you know...It pushes you in that mode like you go out and lime with the bad boys."

He said he stopped robbing people in his late teens because he saw a lot of his friends going to jail or dying and he did not want that to happen to him. He saw both sides of the life, and as a man with no charges, he had a chance to get out of it. "I dun off with that and start working," he explained.

"The temperament of a young person is different. The temperament is stronger. As a teenager, if we want something from you, and you do not give it up, as a young person we would wring something in you.

"I had another friend that I taught that life to and eventually I told him leh we done with that and he said 'Nah! I gotta eat!' and that same night the police hold he and I did feel bad, cause I tell he 'My man, we gotta done with that'- but you get to the point that you would done but other people will always want to carry it on.

"Nowadays you can't just say you done with that life because nobody ain't forgetting you and nobody ain't care."

He said that he saw a lot of his friends from the Orleans who had carried on in that life had died.

"You could done and say you gine live a different life and tell the men you done but then the person you did wrong gine study you and come and kill you...they will always remember and come for you. In the past, the men would say live and let live and move on."

He views involvement in crime and violence as a "disease" – a disease, which in his opinion affects black people moreso than any other race. He doesn't see it changing anytime soon. "It won't change. It is worse than [the] Corona [virus]!

"It's now not only the poor but the rich and who have education that are shooting the guns and getting involved. The wealthy ones are the ones who have the influence over the youth, as well as the elders providing the guns. If you are not financially fit you would always have to look for someone in a higher place to help. **As long as you ain't working on your plan you have to work on somebody else plan** and bow to them so that they can help you.

"Only certain people used to have guns and move with guns and only certain people used to give people guns ...all like my bredren had a lot of guns and he promised he would never give me a gun cause of my mindset. He know if I get one I gine go in jail and sit down long cause if anybody do me anything, I am going to harm them!"

He also said that in the past he had seen persons get shot for fifty dollars. He pointed out that drugs are not the main problem with all the violence.

"It's the petty things, because you would go jail and you and a man would have a disagreement in jail and you from one side and he from one side. He would bring that out of jail, cause back in my day when one man interfere with me, we gine come for you. We don't care how much people you around - we gine come for you. We ain't want them. We want you … but nowadays it ain't like that …it's like if I from Christ Church and you from town, and me and you got a lil vibe, is like the whole of Christ Church against the whole of town - that is how it is now. People joining up and plotting against one another.

"Men does see men and just don't like them and just want to kill them".

He stated that the Orleans had always carried a stigma. "Men does think that youngsters in the Orleans now cruel but them ain't as cruel as the elders that used to chop ya up and beat ya up bad."

Even though the Orleans always had that stigma, he stressed that it is a happy place. "The Orleans community are defenders and the people don't talk to people or share information easily. They don't look for trouble, they don't deal with the police and the hardest place you could get information from is the Orleans," said the young man.

"People realize they don't need one another because they have guns. I have goons and shooters, so I break off. So the crews break off from each other, and then you get inside wars where people break off from each other within the group.

"It then comes down to if you from one side, stay on that side and don't cross that line unless you are strapped."

He made an interesting observation. He said within each group or gang are bad apples and upstarts, who are always looking for war. What he essentially was saying was that while most of the gang or group were overall about peace unless they were attacked, there were always the "lone rangers"; some referred to them as "loose cannons" who go and initiate wars or always want to fight or shoot. In his opinion, this is a major issue. "Both sides have upstarts who start other upstarts, and start a war between communities."

He then spoke about the dilapidation in The Orleans. "This is due to neglect. Government won't look at people in The Orleans. When you take a look at the Orleans around 3- 4 pm, you don't see anyone. It is the same in Chapman Lane. The war takes so much out the ghetto, that it leaves them with nothing. Also, a lot of people don't like one another. If they did, why would they give them a gun to put themselves in trouble?"

CHAPTER FOURTEEN

Community Urchin To Community 'Boss'

His father died when he was two years old, so he never knew a father. His mother had 7 children and worked as a domestic. His first job was as a gas station attendant in Baxters Road, but he did not last a week because on the second day, his boss sent him out for lunch and on the third day one of the supervisors sent him for lunch, all this within his lunch hour. "I asked them if this was part of my job description and they fired me!"

In the 1970's, when he was just 14 years old, his sister and mother migrated to the USA leaving him with three brothers in a house. "You think anybody can tell me come back? Nobody there could tell me come back," he said. "I had to hit the streets hard! I had to live my life as it came."

Life had very little structure. He began hanging out around the shops and bars with the older men. He used to dive in the wharf for money. His schoolmates started putting money in his mouth and saying to him "Looka B..". He said the Harbour Police would try to steer the speed boat at him when he dived.

"That is when I threw away pride and industry and just lost any care in the world," he said.

He started smoking marijuana, claiming that it started coming in the late 1970's. According to him, back then there was a Trinidadian man who was able to bring in drugs through the customs.

He grew up in poverty where there was never enough money to buy food or pay a bill. He made the point that he was never privileged to have anyone in society doing anything for him. Having to choose his own path to survive, he started frequenting Bridgetown with the sole purpose of stealing. However, he noted that even from a young age, he was always seen as a leader amongst all his people, and as a consequence, many of them brought their problems to him. Yet, he lamented that there was no one to whom he could take his own problems.

He argued that in society, people think that the ghetto people bring guns into the country, but was quick to point out, "Where do or can we get money from to bring in guns?"

He opined that some merchants realised that men would pay anything for a gun, so they started bringing them in among their imported goods.

"We have a tendency of using one another to look good. I can't get a customs officer to work for a poor black ghetto man unless you become successful - what they will do with me is use me to look good, so I can't bring nothing through the airport or seaport. Every move I make 'they' are recording it, but when police hold drugs, they not reporting it. What they doing now is they making enemies for you and the people overseas that you doing business with, because you can't tell a man [overseas] that his drugs get hold especially when there is nothing mentioned in the press. So they are making war between you and your suppliers. People will get killed for it."

He added, "There are people that die hard, that work by the book. There are people that are cool that will say they don't want to unfair anyone because they don't want anyone unfair them. Then there is the dog that don't care what you do, there's always a problem for you. He will hunt you down, run you down, try to kill you.

"The police do not care who kill who in these ghettos until they touch the fabric of high society. If they start robbing stores or banks, that is where you will see the big headlines and they will search every house in Barbados, but as long as we don't touch that fabric of society and keep killing one another, that is what will make the system roll," he stated emphatically.

"The robbers of the people keep glorifying themselves. In order to glorify themselves, they always have to have somebody to point their finger at."

He referred to the *Scarface* movie starring Al Pacino when the main character says, "You need people like us, so you can have someone to point your fingers and say there is the bad guy!"

He admitted that cocaine gave him everything and then took it back. He lost his freedom; he lost everything. He vowed that when he came home from prison, he was going to change. But that change proved even harder than when he was first out there hustling! He also did not want his children to do the things that he did.

He said if he got "a little weed", he would deal with it but at the end of the day he was not doing anything unless he was the boss.

The 1980's were "sweet", according to him. Whatever was going on had to come through him as the boss. There was nothing going on in the illegal business of which he was not made aware. There was very limited competition back then.

"I was looking at millions. I always wanted to be a millionaire! Never dream small - always dream big! I can't do petty hustling or petty stealing, nothing so. If I have $5.00, I have to give you back, because the kind of money I want now, $5.00 is a joke."

Back in his glory days, he said, he could have called his Spanish connection in Venezuela and tell him just drop some product in Grenada and he would have his speedboat or fishermen collect it. He even recalled an occasion when they moved drugs right next to a church, while the service was going on.

Back then, there was no tension with the police. "Whatever the police found, you were allowed to go along with," he said.

His money started to increase and he could afford lawyers.

Untouchable?

"I started every Saturday with a bag of money and give away $10 and $5 and pay the poor people's light bills, water bills, send school children, buy bicycles for the youth etc." He said that his community then was "the fastest weed and cocaine block in Barbados," and that he was untouchable. Everyone had to come to him for whatever it is they wanted, he asserted.

This was also when he caught the attention of the police! The police started to see him 'flossing' with his money. He started wearing a lot of jewellery and investing in vehicles and businesses which drew their attention. "They also saw when people got into trouble, I would bail them out."

He claimed that he was one of the persons responsible for the eventual creation of a dedicated Drug Squad.

"There was a Coast Guard Unit, but it was not big and they could not patrol the whole area. The police were not involved in patrolling the waters either. Police would take away the drugs and sell it back to you. When the higher police authorities started to realise that this was happening, they formed a Drug Squad."

He said that the police were also not so 'hip' as to what was going on as they are now. "The police now have drones and specific people that would target men. For example, they just want to hear that Charmaine is running drugs for a particular area and they will have men target Charmaine, having her under surveillance," he stated.

In his words, he tried to "get legal." However, according to him, the authorities said "this man is getting too far" and they started targeting him. He made a few slip-ups and ended up incarcerated.

He was caught with 250 pounds of weed, which was worth about $600,000.00 at the time.

When asked for his opinion on how the streets have changed since his time, he said that what saddens him is that he can remember decades ago when people referred to each other as queens and kings, princes and princesses, but that no longer happens.

"From in the 1990s, the culture became dirty. The American culture has changed that. Rap music started out by singing about the struggle like KRS1 and Coolio. The big record companies told them that they could make millions, but people do not want them singing about the struggle.

They want them to sing about bitches, whores, guns, killing one another, disrespecting one another." He said Barbadian culture adopted this music and "swallowed the swag, and we swallowed how they do it too".

"This drug game is nothing that you can trust right now. There is no loyalty, no trust on the streets. From the time you have men calling one another dogs, bitches and disrespecting women, it could never ever be any good.

"Another thing that is serious is that nobody is teaching young people how to transform from being a child to an adult with responsibilities such as paying bills, running a house and so on. That is why we are seeing a lot of the wickedness we are seeing today! You have young people between 17 and 23 years old who do not know how to be responsible for anything!"

It pained him to see that the ghettos are now full of members of what he referred to as the "brainless gang" - young girls and boys walking the streets all hours of the day and night. He said the COVID pandemic made it worse, where mothers, afraid of catching COVID or spreading it to others, left their homes to go and live elsewhere and leaving their children in the house unsupervised.

He said that many of the young men are too willing to take up a gun and shoot someone without any questions.

"If you come out here with two guns and a man to shoot, men glad to shoot somebody because you know what they want? They want to hold on to one of those same guns to be powerful because that's the only power they have. The only power we have out here is if a man has drugs or money, or if he has guns. The only thing people respect in these areas is money or violence. This is what has been bred in these communities.

"Love doesn't live here. In fact, love does not even live in mainstream society. Everyone has an attitude. Even driving on the streets, you can see the rage among people."

He believes the rage comes because people have come to realise that "the system is a lie".

INCEST AND DRUG ADDICTION

The scourge and the fuel

Even though this book primarily explores gang culture, incest and drug abuse from all strata of society are also significant dimensions of our unspoken truths. These crimes and their deleterious effects on their victims are two aspects of Barbadian society that are spoken of in hushed tones.

In the following two chapters, we will read of two individuals: Janet, a 26-year-old incarcerated female who has been a victim of multiple instances of incest and who ended up in prostitution; and Trent, a white 37-year-old male who shared the impact of drug addiction on his life. Like the other persons in this book, they too were searching for something. In Janet's case, she lacked love, direction and guidance. In Trent's case, it was a strong desire to fit into a specific social construct fueled by curiosity.

The influence of peer pressure, which is a common denominator in most of the persons interviewed in this book, is also noted.

The two individuals will speak about their challenges and how the experiences have shaped their lives.

CHAPTER FIFTEEN

Janet: How Incest Scarred Her Life

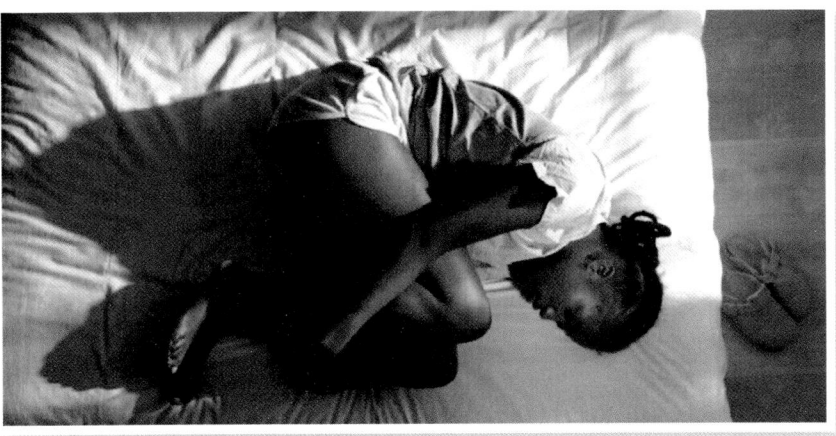

Rape is one of the most heinous crimes a person that one can commit against another. It is invasive, demeaning and personal. The emotional scars can last a lifetime, and they can cripple the victim in every sphere of his/her existence.

When the rape is perpetrated by a family member, the reprehensible violation is even worse. Incest is one of the most unreported crimes because it exposes dark, dirty family secrets. However, the victim suffers and like any other rape victim, can be scarred for life. It is hard for most people to fathom how a father, brother, uncle, grandfather or even a female family member can be sexually attracted to their kin. Unfortunately, it happens, and in Barbados, it happens more often than most of us would prefer to believe - it is another one of the unspoken truths.

Janet, just like many of the men referenced in this book came from a dysfunctional home and was looking for security, love, and relevance which were not available at home. The difference between Janet and the men referred to, is that she is a female and instead of being treated as a recruit, she became a target for predators.

Janet's story is one that is very hard to come to terms with. She is only 27 but has had a very difficult life – a life that most people cannot imagine even surviving such. Janet, the mother of two children, is a victim of incest, with all the males in her family having sex with her from the time she was a child – her father, four brothers, a cousin and a step-father.

She has spent almost all her life as a victim of incest. Her parents were no longer together, and her mother spent a lot of time away from home, working to provide for her family of eight. The family was as dysfunctional as far as the term "dysfunction" could be used descriptively. They fought often among themselves, moved around a lot, and incest was the family's dirty secret. Her brothers had sex with all her sisters, and she, being the youngest, suffered the most and the longest.

Her cousin also had sex with her, but she was afraid to report it to the police because of whom her cousin knew. She also believed that the police would do nothing.

Her father raped her for years. "My father did not live with us. I was the only one of my siblings who was his child. He would get drunk, come and collect me, take me to his house, have sex with me, make me bathe, throw money at me, carry me back home and threaten to kill me if I told anyone about what he was doing," Janet recounted. This sexual abuse by both her father and her brothers went on for years, until she was 17 years old.

Eventually, the family's dirty secret became public. The sexual abuse not only affected her but her sisters as well. One of her sisters ended up smoking crack cocaine and was in drug rehab. Most of the children left as soon as they turned 16. As the sisters grew older, they began to speak of and share their experiences. . One sister divulged what they had all been suffering for years to others outside of the family.

Around the same time while Janet was entering her teenage years, she was becoming rebellious; and would run away at every opportunity. She confided in her friend, who told Janet's horrible story to another friend. She was placed in a children's home; but Janet would run away even more often. "I ran away to wherever my feet took me!" However, whenever Janet ran away, she would promptly be reported missing. People would see her, and she would be brought right back to the home.

Social services became aware of the other incest cases within the home and the Child Care Board intervened and it became a court case. Janet, after leaving the children's home, grew up in different places, including living with a friend of the family.

From a very early age, Janet said that she was heavily involved in the partying scene. "Sometimes, I would sneak out through the window in the middle of the night with my sisters and go partying, smoke marijuana or snort cocaine and drink alcohol." One night her mother caught them and boarded up the window.

Unfortunately, Janet never had a good relationship with her mother whom she considered too strict; she felt unable to talk with her as a daughter should. Janet believes that her mother's busy schedule created the perfect situation for abuse to occur within the home.

This constant daily physical and emotional battering to which Janet was subjected, fueled tremendous anger and resentment within her, to the extent that she acted out at school, often getting into fights because of the family dysfunction.

"I was always angry, would always pick fights or I would run away. I also liked to see blood when I was fighting because I wanted to hurt people who come around me with foolishness," Janet stated.

She was sent to the juvenile detention school, Summervale, after getting suspended for fighting at secondary school. She spent a year at Summervale; was returned to her home and got into trouble again for wandering. She was then returned to Summervale the following year.

When questioned why she did not seek counselling, she said that she often told herself she didn't need counselling. "You have to harden your heart," she said.

At 17, she moved out of her home. One day she decided to skip school and went to a "sugar daddy", who took her in, and from then she moved in with him and was living there. The sugar daddy had diabetes but he took care of her, she said.

On the streets, she would turn to anyone who told her she could be anything she desired and that she was beautiful. These things made her feel good.

Self harm

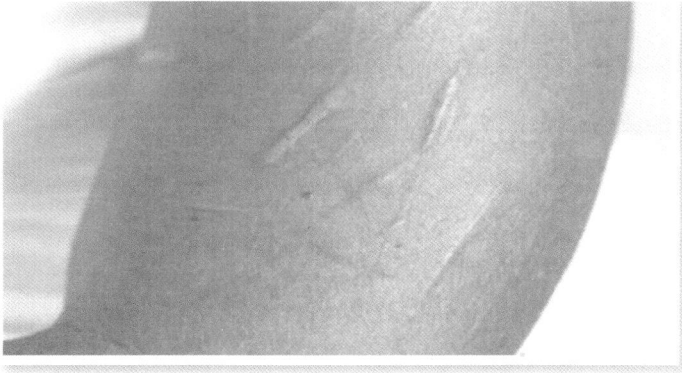

When one takes an immediate glance at Janet, you will see scars all over her body, especially her arms. Janet was self-harming from the time she was 15 years old and in detention at Summervale. She would break the glass in the window of the institution and deliberately cut herself with the broken pieces. She revealed that authorities in Summervale put her down in the 'hole' for months for defacing the property. "If you do me something and I feel hurt, I would cut myself to feel better When someone does me something, I want to see blood. Seeing blood brings calmness." Each cut was for a person who hurt her, she revealed.

Challenging God

She got pregnant at 17 years old by a man she met while prostituting and the man forced her to have an abortion. She said she was devastated and cut her pregnant belly, feeling no sympathy or regret for her action or possible harm to the baby. "I cut my belly while pregnant as a sign that the child is an abomination," she said wryly. She proceeded to have the abortion.

She started to ask herself what was wrong with her. She started to question God. People ask about a God, she said but she asked how can a God who was supposed to protect her, allow this to happen? It was too much. "I was an innocent girl who never saw a star pitch yet! God, how can you let an innocent girl suffer?"

Janet wanted to hurt people when her father and brothers raped her. She stressed that it was for this reason alone that she pushes people away and deliberately hurts their feelings because she doesn't want to let her guard down and become vulnerable.

Admitting that this was not an overnight feat, she said it took her years to harden her heart, and now it is hard. "I love people from a distance," she stated.

From a young age, after her sexual abuse started, she also started to like girls because men changed her mind from wanting them. "I used men sexually," she readily admits. "But I don't love men, I love women. I believe women are right for me. Women give me a euphoric feeling – a feeling I never experienced with a man."

Referring to men as 'sperm donors', she did say that she had always wanted children "to show them the love I never had".

Street culture – working on the streets

Janet is familiar with the street culture. She started using drugs from 13 years of age and said that her father introduced her to her first drink and first smoke. "My father rolled my first spliff for me," she said. He also told her that if she wanted to smoke, she had to roll her own spliff (marijuana joint).

As she started to work on the streets, Janet started to use party drugs such as ecstasy and mollies. These drugs made her "hyper and do foolishness".

Drugs also gave her more energy and more sex appeal. "It is a seductive feeling," she said. "It will keep you going for the whole night." She said she liked popping pills because it gave her an adrenaline rush. "If you slow down, you feel your heart rate going down." She also would do drugs with her clients, and recalled a client who used to pay her to pipe with him.

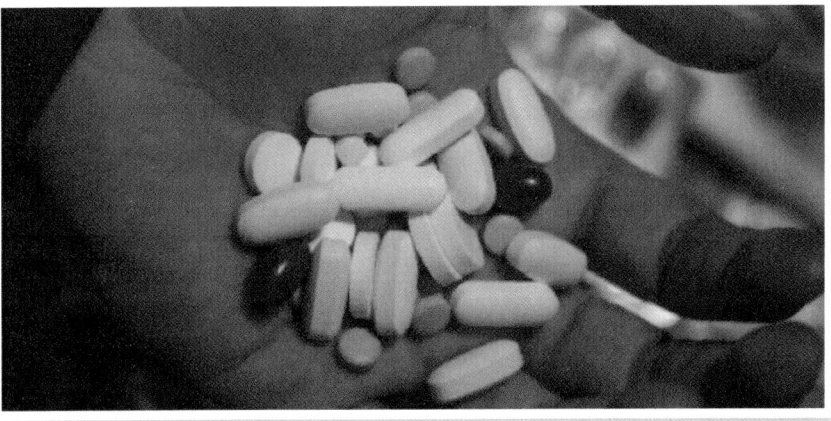

Yet she stressed that she was never addicted to drugs. She maintained that only "weak-minded people" get addicted to drugs. "Drugs is not my addiction, sex and money are."

Money was her love. She emphasized that she wanted to star in a blue movie and "sell [her] soul", even though she did not quite explain how she was going to sell her soul. Janet's only reason for not doing such was because she did not want it to affect her children. However, she then claimed that if prison did not happen, she would have "gone into blues".

How Janet became involved in prostitution

She recalled how she started to associate with a group called the Panty Pudding crew and at just 15 years old, to meeting a prostitute, who shall be called Shandy. She and Shandy had a conversation one day while she was high on drugs, and Shandy told her, "I like you and I like your vibe. You would do good on the streets. You have what it takes to make it in the streets."

Shandy gave her what she considered sage advice. "If you giving it away, give it way for something. Never lay down in need and wake up in want." Janet liked the idea and started prostitution.

"The streets welcome you when you are young".

So at 15 years old, Janet started working on the streets. "I started doing house calls," said Janet. "Shandy then started hooking me up and got a share of the money I was making. Shandy would hook me up with "big men: married men and influential clients."

She said that married men were different and "freaky", and loved to talk. "They want to talk to you about their life before they do business, but they also wanted to do a lot of freaky things, like choking you, role-playing with them, wanting you to urinate on them and walking them like dogs and other BDSM activities," she recalled.

When she turned 17, she started dancing in clubs. She said that on a good night, she would make $2,000.00. She lived that life for 4 years until her incarceration. She lived lavishly, and spent the money wildly. She supported her children and made sure "mummy good." She said that her mother knew that she was prostituting her body, but did not care as long as she was receiving money as well.

She explained her hatred of men. She suffered physical, verbal and emotional abuse from men whom she thought loved her. "Men would tell me that I was beautiful, and they knew I had low self-esteem and was trying to build courage." She said her clients would call her a whore, bring other women for her to have sex with, force her to join in with them and other women. If she did not comply, "it would be licks!" she said with a laugh. They would choke her, slap her in her face, tie her up, and do other depraved acts to her body. She recalled that her hatred for men was so strong, that she wanted to invest in a car and "lick down men with it".

She said she has been choked, gun butted, handcuffed, and kept in captivity for nearly a week among the other scores of atrocities committed against her. She recalled that one day, after her abortion, she wanted to leave home and went to visit the guy she was seeing who happened to be a security guard. He started to kiss her over her body. Then suddenly, without warning, he handcuffed her. "He was possessive," she said. He tied her up for 5 days. "He would come and undo me to go to the toilet and then he would feed me.

"I had to get away from him. He would stalk me, beat me, leave me with black and blue eyes, lip swollen…. The licks were like Mike Tyson! I thought a man beating you meant he loved you." When some of the men she was involved with hit her, they would come and tell her they didn't mean to hit her, but that she had made them do it.

Janet states that it was only after she came in to prison that she saw her worth. She always saw herself how people saw her – a whore, worthless and that nobody would want her. She recalled her own mother told her she would never be anything good, even though she herself was a chronic alcoholic.

Janet thought about suicide many times in her life. She told herself life was not worth it. She took an overdose of pills on several occasions, including the diabetic pills of the old man with whom she was living. In the interview she admitted that some days "I still can't take life anymore."

She made the point that men on the streets are putting their women on the market, and making other men or women have sex with them. "They don't care about love no more these days. Women are going ahead because they think the men love them. The men keeping the majority of the money and giving the women what they think they are worth."

Janet is still haunted by the incident that caused her to be imprisoned. She suffers from depression and is on medication.

Her advice to women (and men) who have been through trauma in life is simply this: "Giving up is not an option. You may not see the bigger picture now but it is worth not giving up."

Janet's life story is indeed a sad and disturbing one. She has been exploited all her life, both by her male family members and then by her lovers and clients. Women like Janet who suffer from low self-esteem due to life's circumstances become easy targets for men who see such women as easy bait to exploit.

As indicated at the beginning of this chapter, Janet's needs were not dissimilar from many of the men in this book. The major difference however, is that the security available for young males in the gang structure is glaringly absent for vulnerable young females such as Janet.

Note: *Victims of incest tend to have a myriad of psychological issues as part of their life situation. Research states that many go on to hurt other people, have sexual dysfunction and become sex workers or drug addicts. Many others suffer from other forms of pathology in their lives. Janet's case is typical of the outcome of rape and incest.*

If you have been a victim of incest or any form of sexual abuse, or know or suspect anyone who has been victimised, please call the Sex Crimes and Human Trafficking Unit of the Barbados Police Service at (246) 430-7333 or the Crisis Hotline at the Business and Professional Women Club in Barbados at (246) 435-2222.

CHAPTER SIXTEEN

"How Drug Addiction Almost Killed Me"

The drug trade is seen as a lucrative business where persons can get rich easily. Drugs such as marijuana, cocaine, methamphetamines, heroin and date drugs such as ecstasy are common on the Barbadian streets. However, there is the downside of the lucrative business – addiction, despair, hopelessness and destroyed families. Here, Trent, a former drug addict – Caucasian and from a wealthy family - who has been clean for approximately a decade shares his story about how drugs almost took his life in the late 1990's and early 2000's.

He stressed that he did not initially get drugs on the streets; his addiction started in suburbia Barbados. He was introduced to drugs at house parties "in the heights and terraces; in houses with automatic gates and big vehicles such as Audis and A-class Benz".

He noted that while the stereotypical image of the drug addict is the decrepit junkie begging on the streets or lying in the gutter, there are several other addicts whose social position makes them less visible, less targeted and even less accessible.

By his own addiction, he was an "undercover addict". His family, friends and employers did not know what he was doing. His two very separate lives took a heavy toll on him.

"I was a functioning addict, meaning I went to work every day like normal, but it was a real challenge." He was torn between two worlds, which made him depressed. He had to give up his habit during the day and function in the workplace; but he couldn't wait to get home to get the high he craved. He was basically juggling his public and private life.

"We used to get meth and cocaine from a prominent business family." He would go to parties in a particular posh neighbourhood on the south coast and get these drugs. Trent described these parties as appearing to be like any normal house party. However, while most persons were socialising at the front, the real party was at the back in a separate room.

In the back room, there would be a great deal of cocaine on the table and one could sniff/consume as much as one wanted.

He admitted that it started to take over his life. He had to remove himself from certain people, places and things to survive because he considered killing himself. "I was so overcome with this addiction, spending $4,000.00 on a Friday night in a certain nightclub in Barbados. The cocaine distributors would party in the club and blend in. They would all go in the bathroom and conduct the transaction. He would snort it on the top of the toilet tank, using a plastic card to line it up and snort it with notes.

"The addiction was overpowering me," he admitted.

"You gone to a fete, but you in a bathroom de whole night just snorting r**hole cocaine off the toilet tank." He said he tried not to bring his addiction home, but his mother knew something was wrong and she told him a while after, that she had premonitions of coming out of her bed, and finding him hanging in the garage. He told her, "Mum, it is funny that you would say that because that is exactly what I was going to do!"

What stopped him from killing himself? His daughter. He felt that if he took his life, his daughter would go to school and her peers would taunt her. He told himself "If you don't care about yourself, at least care about your family."

He said that some nights he would even go into the drug 'holes' where he stuck out like a sore thumb because of his race. "They knew I was coming for drugs, simply because of my race. There was no other reason for me to be in these areas," he said.

"You descend to a level that is socially below you."

He said he was too proud for rehabilitation and he decided to rehabilitate himself. "I made a conscious decision to help myself".

Admitting that it was the hardest thing he ever had to do, he said it took him nearly a decade to clean himself of his addiction.

"I suffered so much in that period to get off drugs and suffered more to break myself totally.

"It's like dealing with an ex-woman. You and she done, but you are still [having sex with] her. It is like dealing with her, and every man that she is having sex with is just haunting you, and you are having sex with other people, but still having sex with her and she's having sex with them and it is confusing you. It was like that with me."

Referring to the term 'recreational drugs', he was adamant there was no such thing. "From the time you try it, especially if it is good quality, you will be hooked and enslaved by it.

"I remember being up for four days straight. You can't sleep. You also did not want to bathe because bathing would damage that high." He would bathe before he got high or not bathe at all.

Then the withdrawals were horrible. "When you go through a withdrawal, you get depressed over miniscule things - like dropping a glass makes you cry," he said, while cringing.

"I took cocaine, methamphetamine... I was frighten for heroin, but God knows I wanted to try it. I used powdered cocaine but I preferred liquid cocaine because I liked it in orange juice."

He knows other men that were in big businesses that were addicted to cocaine and other hard drugs and still cannot get off these drugs.

He said that they are "untouchable" because of their social status and connections. "Do you know who has them untouchable? Black people, not white people. Black people enable them to disable everybody else."

"You live in Barbados where there are 95% black people. You cannot operate any successful business, organization, not even a f**king lucky dip without influence or input from black people."

As it related to the method used to transport drugs in Barbados, Trent believes fishing boats are still bringing in drugs. A friend told him about going off Tobago and meeting the boats. His friend said he had a gas bottle with the bottom cut out and he would stuff it with cocaine. The Coast Guard would come and check the boat in the Careenage and check EVERYTHING but the gas bottle. He would then take up the gas bottle in front the Coast Guard officers and walk off the boat. His friend revealed to him that he had been bringing in cocaine in gas bottles for years.

There are also over the counter pills that people in Barbados are getting high on. Xanax is a sedative, but it makes you feel good. You can get cough syrup into methamphetamines. Cough syrup and other medication like ibuprophen are used to make meth. While not many people use this form of medication to get high, they apparently use acid.

"People are addicted to it here. It is a raw form of ecstasy. Party scenes were and still major hubs for ecstasy. You can get any drugs here, even an expensive drug named crocodile," he stated.

He never really liked smoking cocaine, stating that he didn't like the high smoking cocaine gave me. He preferred pill popping and snorting. Regrettably, he said it destroyed the septum in his nose.

"If I was smoking, I would get a snap brandy bottle and bore a hole in the bottom with a nail, get brillo pads and wash out the soap, and stuff the top and get a lighter and burn the cocaine rock on to that, and smoke it through the back.

"Eventually over time, the bottle would turn white, so you can't get cocaine now - you high and crazy because all you are studying is where you will get more cocaine from.

"You take the bottle and put some water in it, shake out the water, put it on foil paper and put the foil paper in the sun and then you lick the residue off. "You become a dog – a fucking paro. That is a 'prickle' move," he painfully recalled.

Trent said that his hearing and level of awareness were amplified a hundredfold while on drugs. "I can hear the hair on my arms blowing in the wind. By the time I got high, I could hear a fucking rat pissing on cotton miles away. My senses increased 100%. I could hear a siren by the hospital from the east of the island. Everything was loud and bright as ra**hole! I could hear everything and I was nervous."

He also became paranoid. "I would be home by myself and I would start peeping around in rooms and looking around suspicious. I wanted to go in the bush near my house and hide. It is a fucked up thing," he recalled.

He made the telling remark: "The worst thing you can do is have an addiction you can afford. It is the absolute worse. It has a lot to do with who you are around – your peers."

Trent stated that there is a "coterie of persons" that you become involved with while you are a drug user. "You attract unsavoury characters. Your type of friends (friend base) deteriorates."

He stressed that one HAS to remove oneself from such people, places and things in order to get out of drugs. You have to remind yourself that you have a problem. Recall that Trevor said the same thing when discussing his previous relationship as a member of *Jesus and the Disciples*.

Trent's advice: "Explore and recognise your value and your purpose or you will fail. It is mind over matter. You have to have the will and keep away from people that are doing those things or you will be ruined. It is like a cancer – you have to go into remission."

What we have to face is that the gateway drugs are marijuana and alcohol. Alcohol is a major gateway drug because in his circumstance, when he drank alcohol, he wanted to get high. According to him, some men, when they drink alcohol, they want to smoke weed. "You start to feel sick before you feel how you want to feel.

"Hard drugs will make you hype. If you are a performer such as a singer, an entertainer, an athlete, anyone who needs to perform and you take cocaine, meth, ecstasy or heroin, they will improve your performance 100%. You don't get tired, and that is the inherent danger," he stressed.

"If you have a cocktail and I sprinkle some meth in it or cocaine because I want to have sex with you and I get you to that vibe where you don't care, you will give it up to me. That time, you don't even remotely like me but I am there and you have that feeling. Then and there, you want that feeling again. You see sex when you high under dem real drugs? That is the best sex in your fucking life. Your orgasm comes from your fucking toes."

Even though he is off drugs, he still gets itches and he scratches until his skin bleeds. He refers to it as the junky itch.

His advice to persons out there: "Don't even try it. Do not even experiment with it. Guard your drink. Don't let anyone slip you a micky. A micky is drugs in a drink. That can hook you. Drugs is the worst thing in the world. I see it at all levels."

He even lost all his teeth to his drug addiction. "Addiction destroys your teeth," he warned. "Drugs like cocaine and meth are acidic. They change the ph. in your body and make your saliva acid and it corrodes the enamel of the teeth, wearing your teeth down to the dentine and eat them into holes."

"They don't even hurt," he said. "They just break off and you wither away.

"The smell of the drugs seep through your pores, making your body smell like sulphur, the smell you get when you first light a match. **You**

have two good days with drugs – the day you start, and the day you end."

He also wanted to appeal to those who are the drug suppliers and distributors, particularly of hard drugs.

"If the drug dealers have any modicum of care or respect for their fellow man they will stop peddling this poison. Yes, it is a quick way to make a lot of money, but look at the losses. Everything you make out of cocaine, you lose… sometimes even your life."

After all he has endured and survived, he is grateful for life. The lesson learnt is priceless. It has taught him to cherish his own existence and the people around him, and most importantly, to let the ones you love know that you love them.

CHAPTER SEVENTEEN

The Role Of Women In Street Culture

Even though gang and street life are predominantly male oriented, women are involved to some significant degree. While most persons believe that women are mainly associates, it has been established that a small percentage of them are active gang members.

Women were not associated with personal weapon usage. They sometimes tried to discourage conflicts and played an important part in community bonding. However, by having sexual relationships with "the enemy", they were often the ones blamed for provoking conflicts.

The police believe that women act as couriers, carry and conceal weapons and drugs, act as lookouts and are used as bait by using sex and feminine prowess. (Study on Gangs in Barbados, 2016).

There are others on the streets who agree. They believe that women are conduits (one woman referred to them as plugs) that cause a lot of crime. On the streets, men use women to set up men. That is how many men lost their lives on the streets. According to one man, women have no say on the streets. "They are like ornaments for men to walk and show off with." Some are used and abused, and some are even passed around on the block.

A lot of wars are started on the street because of women. Her man would be in prison and another man would [have sex with] her and that would start a war," said one woman from an inner city community. His friends and family would also get involved and start a community war.

There is a significant dimension to the female involvement in gang activity as noted by many: passing information to the enemy when relationships sour.

"A woman would be dealing with a man from [a particular gang] and at the same time, she is dealing with a man from the opposing gang. Then when she and the man get way, she shares information with the enemy and this has started gang wars in Barbados."

There is also the thrill of being involved with a gangster. Some women who were affiliated with the streets and who are currently incarcerated agree. When asked why women got involved with gangsters, one woman explained, "It is done for fame - the thrill of having a bad boy!

"We get protection, full forward and respect by his soldiers and by people on the streets generally."

They agreed that in many cases, women have to share the gangsters or "bad boys", but many do not mind sharing.

"Many times, he has a main woman who is supporting him and is taking care of him, and he shares the money with the other women. So we don't mind, once we getting taken care of too. Some women will give their man a car, give him money to buy things and she knows he has other women. Sometimes, everyone does 'gree. The outside woman has to respect the man's main woman and this is understood among all the women."

"Once I getting my due, I don't care," suggests one woman. At the end of the day it is about fortune and fame or good sex."

Some of these women are actively involved in the street culture. They hide guns and drugs for their lovers, use their legitimate businesses to assist in laundering money for the men and also transport guns and drugs for the gangs. In many cases, they assist or are even up- front in the business because they (the women) know that they are not often the focus of law enforcement.

Parents - particularly mothers - and other female siblings are also active enablers in the illegal activities of their loved ones. One female said "Parents and girlfriends know what is going on. A mother would protect her child at all costs. I even know of a case where a mother gave her child a gun to protect herself. There is the old saying 'I prefer a bad child than a dead child!'"

One community activist makes the point: "If women were more conscious, a lot of things could change. Women have more influence than they seem to understand. A lot of men on the streets have a weakness for women and if women were stronger and more positive and more conscious, it would do something to those men. A lot of those men would take their place because the women have that power to influence them." Unfortunately, many women who are involved with these men do not see themselves like that: they see themselves as pawns of the men.

"It is good to have a gangster; it is high profile to have a gangster," said one man. While admitting that he grappled with why so many decent women got involved with gangsters, he came to the conclusion that it gave them a sense of security: "I with the boss". Similar to what was expressed earlier by the females, he also suggested that a lot of the women liked it for the thrill.

Some females get into relationships and have children with these gang leaders just to be associated with the man and the fame of having his child or to acquire material benefits. "They call themselves 'Gangsta Bitches,'" said one law enforcement officer.

"They are oblivious to the fact that these men's lifestyles can take the same men away from them. They somehow believe they will live forever," said one man.

"Sometimes, people are blinded to simple facts; there is no self-reflection. They do not take the time to sit down and conclude, 'This is not making any sense'. But there is an explanation for this: people's own wants and needs cloud their judgement. This comes from a basic need in individuals.

"Sometimes, you would know that a man is not any good for you, but that basic thing (our own innate desires such as companionship, attention, sex) keeps you there. You know he is treating you bad and he is no use for you, but that basic desire keeps you there. It is like a jungle."

CHAPTER EIGHTEEN

Evolution Of The Streets And Gang Culture

In an extensive 2016 interview with Assistant Commissioner of Police Mark Thompson, now deceased, he stated that in the 1980's, there were entities/groups such as the *CNN* and *Jesus and the Disciples* and though there was and still is no legislation to define them as 'gangs', the RBPF loosely defined them as such. There were other pockets of troublesome groups, but they mostly used to gamble and engage in nuisance crimes. Other troublesome groups were involved in drug running and many of these persons were killed in this type of crime.

Thompson said that forty years later, we still have groups of persons who the police will now define as gangs which have graduated to being heavily into drug trafficking, extortion and firearm crimes. According to law enforcement, the swing has been caused because of the availability of guns and competition (there were not so many players in the drug trade in the 1980's as they are now) leading to turf wars. Organized crime is a "heavier business!"

He also said that the police needed to move towards anti-gang legislation because it was the only way to deal with crime on the blocks. He admitted that if the police had gang legislation, certain cases would have been easier to deal with. The crime sleuth also said that community conditions, such as poverty, enabled the gangs to take root.

"When the official mechanisms do not provide for your basic needs, you go outside these mechanisms," he stated.

"Police and other law enforcement agencies cannot provide these needs," said Thompson. "Dons provide these needs – food, school clothes and a sense of belonging. The Dons buy their loyalty. They socialize the citizens into what they want them to be."

Admitting that this was a challenge for the RBPF, he said that social agencies do not have the resources like these community leaders. "The RBPF has the Anti-Gang unit which has a mandate. It is the only policy that exists with respect to gangs," he explained.

However, he made it very clear at the time that the RBPF will "continue to dismantle, disrupt and engage in social programmes so that people will not be inclined to join gangs."

Interviews with current gang members

Interviews were conducted with current gang members to ascertain why they joined the gang, what is involved in gang life, why there is a current war going on and what is the future for them. Gang members were given fictitious names and will be referred to as Adam, Barry, Cliff and Dennis.

Background of gang members

Adam

Adam admitted to having an anger problem all his life. At secondary school, he got into a fight, hit a student with a piece of wood and knocked out his teeth. He was expelled from school at 15 years old and his life plummeted thereafter. He ended up on the streets selling drugs.

"I grew up in a well-known urban community which has been always badly labelled, and I grew up as part of the street culture. Yes, not everyone who grows up in this community has to be part of the street, but you are either in it or not, and the streets found me."

Without elaborating, he stated that he had been pushed to the limit. "A tank can only take so much before it overflows," he remarked. He is now on remand for murder.

Adam revealed that when he was younger, he wanted to be with the bigger boys and achieve certain 'things'. He started to hustle 'things' and this brought certain "energies" (negative people), to him. He took drugs on consignment from "The Mafia" but then men started owing him, avoiding him or downright refusing to pay him. "You can't owe The Mafia," he said. "When you owe The Mafia, it makes my profits short."

His mindset is "On the streets, when you start something you can't end it."

Barry

Barry is 22 years old and incarcerated. He admitted that he was a shooter and member of one of the current rival gangs. Barry openly confessed that he had a love for shooting. He said that at the age of 13, a man from his community pulled a gun on him and he went to an elder from the same community for assistance. This elder gave him a gun at that tender age and he shot the man after seeing him in a public space. A few years later, he was charged at 16 years old for the use of a firearm, when he shot at two people.

Barry stated that he liked adventure as a youngster. He said he loved killing animals and birds as a child, and would catch lizards and put them to fight each other. He would also catch fowls, cut off their heads and pour the blood in a bucket. He would then catch small fish for bait, and put them in the bucket with the blood. He would then pour the blood water into the ocean to attract fish and then catch them.

When he was around the age of 7 or 8 years old, he would leave home by himself and take walks unknown to everyone. This was odd behaviour for a child at that age.

Throughout the interview, he claimed that his mother disliked him from the time he was born. She was abusive towards him and he did not know why. However, he stressed that he loved his mother unconditionally.

Growing up, he was a bully both at school and in the community. He recounted that he would rob children and other people of their money. "I took away money from children at Coleridge and Parry, Frederick Smith, Alexandra and other schools in the north because my mother never gave me money. If they did not willingly give me their money, it would be problems."

He attended the Frederick Smith school and admitted that he carried to school a .38 revolver from the time he was in 2nd form. Barry claimed that he hit the Principal in his head with a piece of wood and was kicked out of school in 4th form. He said there had been a confrontation between himself and the Principal, because according to him "the Principal tell he self I frighten", so he had to prove a point.

"I came up hard. My mother gave me nothing. I survived by robbing people or shooting people for the gang. I would then give my family money that I earned through these robberies or shootings," he said.

He said that even though his mother did not like him, he gave her money when she was without. She would question him as to where he got his money from. "Don't worry about that, mummy. Just hold this money," he would tell her.

"I moved out from home and used to live in an abandoned house with no roof and slept under the cellar. He kept referring to his girlfriend who took him from those conditions and brought him to live with her. It was then, he said that he knew she loved him. He said for a year, he did not shoot anyone. However, his mother's death proved traumatic for him. It triggered him and he committed eight shootings within the year after her passing!

Cliff

Cliff is one of eight children. He attended the Alma Parris School but left at 15 years old and went straight on the block, where the boss took him under his wing and Cliff began to work for him as a soldier. He was imprisoned two years after leaving school on a murder charge.

Cliff said he tried to take a different route in life, but it did not work because, according to him the system was set up in a way where people who make mistakes in life cannot prosper.

"I tried to get a job, but because a police certificate of character was needed, that did not work out. I had to go the route I know, which is crime."

Loyalty

At the centre of gang involvement is the issue of loyalty and respect. Loyalty is key in the life of a gang member and this was emphasized by every single man interviewed for this book. All members of a gang are supposed to look out for each other.

"In the gang, I practise loyalty and back you whether you are right or wrong," said Adam. "Loyalty means a lot to me. Things that people do for you, you must show gratitude and do things for them.

"Being loyal to the boss is key. Once the boss looks good, you look good."

However, Cliff noted that there are men who get involved in foolishness and who are only looking out for themselves. "These men have different agendas. Men drift to the block because they are looking for love, looking for attention and they find it on the block."

Cliff said his loyalty was so strong, both to the boss and to his friends, that he would shoot people for his friends out of loyalty and respect, and not necessarily for money.

Dennis

Dennis revealed that he was not only a gunman, but that he had a drug problem. He had been raised in a children's home and had moved around from school to school in his earlier years. He had attended Alma Parris School, and later the St George Secondary School. He had left school at an early age. He has never known a mother or father, and admitted to smoking marijuana from the age of 10 years old. He said he had been introduced to marijuana by seeing people smoking.

He later gravitated to cocaine. He was introduced to the drug on a construction site at which he was working. He gave his workmate some money to get something to smoke, and he brought him a blackie. He pulled it a couple of times and liked it; and then became hooked on it by the age of 16.

He also started piping crack with his brother, and according to him it started getting serious. He then started stealing from people to support his habit. He sought help at Verdun House where he stayed for a year.

When he returned to society, he went straight to the block. He then began engaging in criminal activities and became a member of the gang.

Hierarchy within the gang

The block has a defined hierarchy. At the head there is the Boss, (sometimes called 'the Foreman') and beneath him, the soldiers.

The Boss also establishes a hierarchy among the foot soldiers. Moving up from the bottom is the soldier who is responsible for cleaning the block. There is also the soldier responsible for delivering and collecting anything required of the Boss.

There is the 'Enforcer' who carries out the orders of the boss (including committing a murder). Then there is the 'Advisor' who advises the boss and provides intelligence gathering to the organization.

When asked what most men on the block are looking for, the response was:

Money

Power

Respect

One of the reasons men are drawn to the block and, ultimately, are willing to be a part of the gang and to be loyal to the boss, is because the boss does not judge them.

"The boss is down for what you are down for – he does not quarrel with you like your mother or other family members will," said Barry. "You can smoke, have a gun, have weed." However, when reminded that the foot soldiers from different gangs are ultimately warring with each other and ultimately dying, he said stoically, "This game is like real-life chess. We are pawns and easy to replace."

Dennis disclosed that one became a member of the gang by linking with the high echelons within the gang. His block linked with another block boss and he became a member. He then became a member of one of the main gangs. His previous boss is in prison.

As a soldier, he did everything, including shooting people. For doing these jobs for the boss, one was rewarded with money, weed or put up in a hiding place if one was 'hot'. "Girls would come to you, and you would get food.

"My boss sent me to school, gave me money, bought clothes and so on for me," said Dennis. "I therefore gave him my loyalty. If he want someone deal with, I deal with it. No questions asked."

Dennis revealed that he felt nothing about taking a life. He described himself as "heartless" and said killing a human to him was like killing a cat.

Dennis also mentioned that there was a 'Big Boss' whom they only saw when they were partying. "Everyone has guns and ammunition and we are there to make sure that he is right. We act as shields to the Big Boss. The Big Boss is the big man with the money."

The gang members claimed that their source of money was tricking people through drug or gun transactions, robbing people, or working for the boss (foreman). "When the boss rings for you to work, you can be designated to move the product and stash it. We sell the product, buy back more product (whether guns or drugs), and put it back into the venture."

The boss is also judge, jury and executioner in the gang. You, as a solider can be called to 'court' for infractions such as lying to the gang; causing unnecessary heat on the block, starting conflict or doing something that cause the gang to be under surveillance by the police; or getting into trouble.

"In the court, you are tried by the Boss and you can be given lashes with a belt or other devices," said Barry. Punishment can even be death. Some gang members stay after they are beaten, and some don't.

Men join gangs for different reasons. Some join because they are looking for father figures, others join because they are looking for fame, some are looking for protection and others are looking for respect.

Unfortunately, some are forced to align with the gang simply because of a friendship with a member(s) of the gang. For example, person X may not initially be a member of the gang, but may just hang out with persons in the gang as friends. However, enemies of the gang will see him hanging out with the gang and he becomes guilty by association and is targeted. He can then be injured or even killed.

As it relates to the issue of joining a gang for fame, the gang members admitted that some men just want to be known and recognised as someone. This is in line with gang literature which states that for many of the men, they are considered nobodies in mainstream society, and look to the streets to become someone. In addition, men want to be recognised as someone to be feared and respected and not to be played with. As one gang member put it: "If nobody hears about you on the streets as a bad man, they will risk at you. You build a reputation by being part of a gang. Every time someone hears your name ringing, it is good. This is the key to the city."

Cause of wars and gang conflict

Those interviewed stated that one of the Caribbean islands started the war, referencing a certain gang through songs. Then musicians started singing for the gangs and travelling to islands, singing these songs.

"Ego and disrespect are causing a lot of wars," admitted Adam. "Men like to go on 'the Gram' and show off, and it causes many of them to lose their lives. It is disrespect to the order."

One of the gang members interviewed admitted that four inmates were paid to "bore him", but they did not get a chance. However, he was of the belief that at some point, the ongoing war will reach the prison, and men may be injured or even killed as a result.

All of the men believed that the current amendment to the Firearm Act will only make matters worse. The Act states that a first time gun offender can be sentenced to imprisonment for not less than 10 years and not more than 20 years; and a second or subsequent offence be sentenced to imprisonment for life or a lesser term, being not less than 20 years.

Barry believes that some men deserved to be shot and he has no regrets about shooting anyone. "If it's a vibe to pull, I would go and shoot a man and go and chill. I feel nothing after. Everything happens for a reason," he said. I had a Glock 30, which is a .45 on the outside and that is how I got my money. I robbed people or shot people with that gun."

He believed that people were starting wars because their friends were dying and they wanted revenge. "The war can't stop. Too many people died already. It has to continue."

Cliff concurred saying that this war will keep going on generation after generation, and the new firearm legislation will make it worse. In his opinion, the legislation is not fair and everyone deserves a chance. He believed that the powers that be need to look at the fact that there is not enough activity on the island to employ everyone or to occupy the minds of young people.

He is adamant that, whereas in the past, the bosses did things themselves, today the generation beneath him was "getting programmed" by the present bosses to do things.

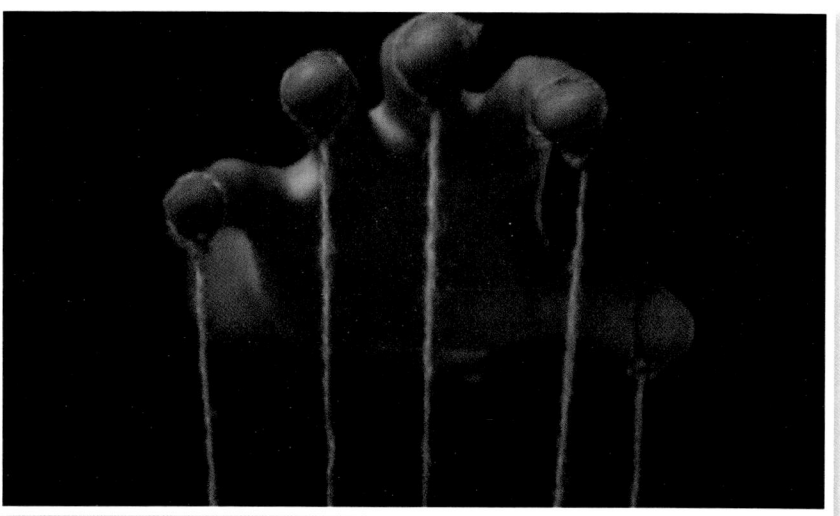

Exiting gang life

When asked about exiting the gang life, the men basically had the same response.

Adam said "I would love to put down my gun, but I can't. I have to protect myself. You don't want to, but people have a past and there are those out there who don't forget that."

Cliff said he cannot put down his gun because he needed it to protect himself. "I prefer to come back here (to prison) than dead," he said matter-of-factly.

"You can't done with that life: that life does done with you!"

All those interviewed have acknowledged that the streets are different now and that gang activity has changed in the past 40 years.

"There is a hierarchy of men and the men that these people see on the streets are at the bottom! The ones at the top are home in their big houses and organizing these things. The men are using ghost chips in cell phones that you cannot trace them."

One man says, "The streets are on another level. The men are not just making money from drugs, they are also into trading on stocks. The men will get men that have smart sense and pay them to do something for them and give them a piece of work. It's all about profit."

The streets are now more technologically savvy. "The men have Facebook. They have Instagram "the Gram". They know this body checking this fete, this person checking this place or gone that place," said one man well into the street culture.

"I can get an enemy killed all now. Hitmen are now a real thing. They are called 'mechanics' – men that fix things. They got men that hungry – always hungry. For these men, life has no value. He wants to go out and he wants to carry out his girl. The leader will tell him 'Hear what gine on. I will give you (random figure) $1200.00 to carry out a hit on a particular man.' That man dead! Believe it, ya dead!" Once the order has been given and the money has passed, the job has to be done.

With reference to revenge killings, this was the sobering response:

"You don't done with that life - that life does done with you!" You get into certain things, if you are a shot-caller, you is a boss, and I out here running your business and I fall into trouble and make you lose money, lost credibility on the street where your operation is in jeopardy, you gine pay for my fucking losses with your life. At the end of the day, all the money has to be accounted for. When the police hold things, and men get lock up in cells, men got to account for that. You are a major leak in the operation. Cos look, you just lost $3 million in weed though. How the fuck you will get over this? We got to get rid of him because he don't have no money.

"In the game, people will value their life but not others. There is no forgiveness. You will forgive a man and he might change his mind and heart and come back and kill you, so it is better that you kill him so that he is terminated and he can't come back...he is now past tense. Kill him. He get buried, go to fuck long. Men will live life like normal, because people mindset have changed. One time a man will kill a man and people will say "Oh, that murder is on your mind and will send you mad.' People change their way of thinking. In their

mindset they believe that if they do something and how the energy and the universe operate, it is fucking right to them, because in their mind and it is how it manifests to them, they are right; even though in other people's mind it may seem wrong.

He went on to say "Anger makes you do things. And sometimes anger makes you do things very smart, especially if the whole job isn't finished and you want to finish the whole job. You ain't gine start smart and end foolish.

"Leaders wear expensive shit, like the Gucci, the Chanel, Versace because they can afford it. The transporters are the men on the motorcycles with the haversacks. Youths also want to dress and look that way. They need funds but won't work a 9-5 for that look.

"You are a youngster that I appreciate. You look like a hustler. I will give you a quarter pound of weed. You will make $6,500.00 offa that. Just give me $2,000.00 and you can keep the rest for yourself. These are the things that lure these men who show appreciation to these leaders Then they add another ¼ pound of weed and work it and make some money. So he is getting respect from this youngster smartly. That youth man would look at him as a savior and tell himself 'that man help me get out the gutter.' The boss man would say the youngster is not good at managing, so all this money he making he gine spend that so fucking wild, that he will come back. The boss don't want him to get bigger than him so he will look for a man that will look clean and spend his money on designer items. A boss will look for a man that manages and put him on his team as a right or left hand and you know, a man that good at money and keep him close."

"The boss is very selective in who he targets. For instance, he would look at a guy and say he hot headed, he don't bluff, he has something to prove to me. He could be a shooter. I will keep him close to me. If I tell he jump there, he will jump there because he wants to show the rest he is better than them. That man would try his best to prove a point. So if anybody barely look at the boss, it can be trouble", said the man.

"The men are also faster to bring harm to you than in past years. There is no more talking, they just will do it."

He said there was one particular gang that was like a heart. However, according to him, this heart had several complex veins running through the country intimately connected to it.

"They overflooding the streets with guns," said one man. Guns in Barbados are expensive. Youngsters cannot afford guns. A Glock 40 starts at $10,000.00. The bosses will give them the guns and control him. Guns are part of your uniform and they are coming in with the weed and dope."

Trafficking on the high seas

Those interviewed revealed that in the past, Barbadian fishing boats would liaise with suppliers from Trinidad and other islands. A rendezvous at sea would be arranged. Barbadian vessels would then go out to meet the supply boat. "You give me your guns and your weed and I hand over your money. We gone fishing and catch fish and load up the icebox and come shore."

They also believe that some luxury yachts are also being used in this trafficking. The private sea-ports, they claim, are being used to facilitate the landing of drugs into the island. "No one is really studying the private sea-ports. These are one of the main ports for smuggling," one man pointed out. The implication of officials in the trade is once again referenced.

Another disclosed the deliberate strategy of diversion. "While a major marijuana drug haul is made in one part of the country that net, say $1 million, you have another massive cocaine landing on another beach that is worth $15 million.

"You see these people holding a lot of fucking weed all the time. Weed is the sacrificial lamb for the importation of cocaine, methamphetamines, speed and ecstasy. Men in Barbados don't make meth; only rich boys in Barbados using meth."

Current day

It is suggested by almost every person interviewed, that there is an ongoing war between two major gangs where one of the gang leaders wants to be the Don of the island. Several of the other blocks and gangs are amalgamating and taking orders from him. When asked why, the answer was simply "for power, ego and greed."

Many of these groupings in Barbados are moving towards syndicates. The Webster dictionary defines a syndicate as "a group of persons or concerns who combine to carry out a particular transaction or project, for example an association of organized criminals."

At the core of this well-organized syndicate is the desire for power. This organization has more manpower, more weapons and more money.

When one investigates the history of American gangs, one notes that this is how it was done. The man with more power and more men expands his territory/turf. It is like international politics. When one possesses more weapons, one invades other territories and takes them over.

A new type of colonialism?

One person argues, "This is slavery all over again. Men taking the rap for weapons. The new ruler is not England and the white man anymore. A particular racial grouping is now in control of Barbados. This is being described as a **new form of colonialism portrayed through gangsterism.** Who are dying? Our black children. Who is losing? Black families.

"Just like in slavery, you give them little trinkets to keep them in line. We will always be the trinket generation – guns, weed, cars, bikes, clothes. They are not getting the house or the land, we are not getting the generational wealth. What generational wealth do any of these men have to show? This grouping has properties left for their children. Estates left for their children, businesses for their children. Repatriating wealth, just like what happened in slavery."

The question was posed: "We are a more educated person than we were two centuries ago. We are in the majority. Why are we sitting back and allowing this modern-day re-enslavement?

The response of one activist was: "We don't have the guns. We don't kill people and get off. They do. Our own people will lock us up and leave them alone.

"Until this dynamic changes, and someone with power says 'I am taking back my community', we will not see change."

Barbadians have now adopted an international gangster culture which is pervasive and portrayed through music. In the music world, the two gangs do not get along, and this has now played out on the streets. "This music is coming from some other Caribbean islands and has now spread to Barbados," notes one law enforcement officer. "In these songs, the men are partying with guns and using gang signs or singing about the gang in their music."

The existing war has created enemies where there were friends; it has infiltrated schools, communities, families, adult and juvenile penal institutions and even social media. The two opposing gangs have musicians who write songs portraying their loyalty to the gang. These songs, some of which are played on local radio stations, are sung by famous deejays who are loyal to the grouping. In popular clubs and parties, these songs are played and, in some cases, they can and do lead to violence. "The music is also making them hit ecstasy and mollies," stressed one incarcerated person.

The prevailing war is essentially playing out the lyrics to the music. This war has created physical boundaries where persons from each group are not allowed to venture into other 'turfs'. To do such is considered disrespectful and can result in loss of life. This situation has become so dangerous and concerning, that it is a threat to law and order in Barbados.

One common thought shared by all those interviewed is that older men are 'programming' the younger men into this way of life by recruiting them, luring them with material items. These men are targeting young boys with no criminal record, taking them out of school (sometimes from as young as 13 years old) and essentially hiring them as young hitmen, giving them $3,000 to kill someone!

These young men care nothing about other people's lives. They are saying they will kill anybody. This is the common view among those knowledgeable about the streets. These youth are coldly calculating that they will be going to jail at a young age and will be out in 10 years and still be young enough to enjoy life on the outside after a jail sentence.

The other issue, in their opinion, is that back in the 1980's-1990's, the gangs like CNN were gaining respect, status, power, fear and held in awe by other gangs and groups. According to one member of the CNN, these younger men are gaining nothing. "The soldiers don't even have a good house to live in, many are still living at their mothers," said one former gang member.

"If I was a boss now, and I had soldiers, all of them would have to have something," said one man. "That is when you know you have loyal soldiers. They don't have loyal soldiers, that is why nuff men run from 'round them."

"A lot of these soldiers these men have are not their original soldiers. Many are new recruits – a lot of young ones that you can push their buttons quick. Once they see a gun, they feel good. That is all they are about – pointing a gun, a pair of hard shoes, get a car and a little weed to smoke."

CNN men said they never used to roll like that. "Everyone shared among each other. We have to be eating good. They just kill people, but they are not eating good."

The former gang members believe that this current war is about who has the biggest guns. "But who is winning, who is getting killed?" they ask.

"Soldiers are the ones killing each other. A lot of them went to school together. What are they killing one another for? Nothing."

In the opinion of the former gang members, it is because one man says he is from one gang, and the other says he is from another gang and one says the other must die because of who they say they represent.

"Back in the day, when someone does you wrong, you as a child would go and complain. Nowadays, the children are taking matters in their own hands," said one person.

There used to be inter-school wars – conflict between one city school and another school from the north. Nowadays, there are no inter-school wars – now the school is a site within which there are school children in rival gangs warring!

We are indeed living in different times.

CHAPTER NINETEEN

Social Exclusion And The Street Culture

"Tried to get a job today but

When dem see my application

Dem say

"If this is really where you reside

Please step outside."

She asked them why

And they replied

"We don't want no trouble

We don't want no trouble, no way.

Lady, where you come from

People die there everyday

For our safety, that's where you should stay."

~ Etana, 'Wrong Address' (2008)

You may be wondering why there is a chapter on social exclusion in a book on gangs and street life. My response is you <u>cannot</u> write a book about the streets without addressing the often embarrassing and shunned topic of social exclusion and alienation, which is one of the drivers of street and gang culture.

It must be emphasized that in low-income urban communities, most young men are **_not_** involved in gangs and do not use serious interpersonal violence against other young men or women.

Social exclusion is the issue of people being excluded and consigned to the margins of society, and while it can be an uncomfortable discussion, it is an imperative and most urgent one.

Social exclusion means in addition to suffering material want, facing curtailed life and vocational options. It means being keenly aware that one is being denied access to status, goods, education, jobs and respect. Social exclusion also means unmet needs for adequate housing, sanitation, education, health and services. Growing up in some communities means too little school and too few jobs and especially for some young men, it means few options for achieving a respected, socially recognised masculine identity apart from gang involvement (Barker, 2005).

Barker addressed the issue of social exclusion as being linked to the economic challenges experienced in the Caribbean since the 1980's.

He stated that every island suffered in that time period since they heavily depended on one or two exports. It was a precarious position.

According to him, structural adjustment policies led to a decline in government spending on many social services such as education and health services. Some may argue that it also affected poverty alleviation programmes as well. They suggest that these economic and political failures left Caribbean young men with little hope and little belief in programmes or initiatives to make a difference in their lives.

Barker also emphasized that many die young because they are trying to live up to certain models of manhood and dying to prove that they are real men.

The rise of the Don, Shotta or Community Leader

Research on crime and social exclusion shows that in some low-income areas – the garrison communities of Kingston, Jamaica, the comunas of Medellin; inner city areas in the United States and some blocks in Barbados – gang leaders are seen by many young people as homegrown heroes. Barker argues that these groups attract mostly marginalised young men to versions of manhood which involve the use of violence as a means to cope with their sense of social exclusion.

As would be noted throughout this book, gang-involved young men are sought after as sexual partners by young women and emulated by other young men. They hold power, have money in their pockets and, by their willingness to use violence against rival groups or gangs, they have **status.**

To be a drug *don* in a Kingston garrison community or the *boss* or *shotta* in some communities in Barbados is to have a name and clout in a setting where many young people perceive themselves to be excluded and disenfranchised.

The local authorities' seeming abandonment of certain communities creates a power vacuum, and this space is filled by gangs, 'dons' and community leaders according to a 2011 paper on *Gangs, Violence and Governance* from UWI, St Augustine. The paper suggests that these communities are caught in a "complex and reciprocal system of protection and clientelism and that members of the gangs are often an integral part of the community."

The Don, gang or community leader often provides money and financial support for individuals or institutions in the form of an alternative welfare system. These alternative forms of governance also settle disputes and try to build legitimacy.

What is important to note is that while violence is not caused by poverty, interpersonal violence *flourishes* in conditions of poverty and social exclusion.

More significant than poverty though is the issue of income inequality. Violence seems to be the highest in communities where too few wealthy individuals control the lion's share of the goods and resources and the poor majority has access to less than its fair share.

Some communities like the Pine, New Orleans, Chapman Lane, Reed Street, Greenfield, Nelson Street, Baxters Road, and Silver Hill at some point have suffered from or continue to suffer from social exclusion and labelling.

One New Orleans resident interviewed for this book said, "the stigma was so bad that people living in 10th Avenue, Orleans would say they live in Kensington as the entire area up to Kensington Oval was considered Kensington on title deeds."

"Business places would stigmatise and label residents and would not want to hire them," said another resident of the Orleans.

This stigma expanded to other communities. The resident of the Orleans said, "If you were from the Pine, Orleans, Chapman Lane, Greenfield and so on, you were considered a devil." Some residents reported that such postcode stigma also presented great difficulties in getting their children into certain schools. It is important to note here that this problem is not unique to Barbados.

One former gunman who left Barbados due to the ongoing war said, "From the time you born in certain parts of Barbados, your path is written. Some people realise too late after 6 or 7 gun charges and can't get anything done in Barbados.... When you put a man in jail, a man can't get a job, he can't get certain things... when this man come out of jail, what you think this man will go and do? Link with somebody that into crime. They are not building a barrier around the foolishness that is going on.

"I come up in a fucked-up environment. I never lacked mummy or daddy, but the company I kept, the place, the surroundings...people looking in already had us classed as vagabonds. I come from a place that bare badness goes on, so from the time people hear that they say 'Oh he will come out to be nothing, he will be just like the rest.'

"If you born in a strip club, what is the first thing you will learn to do? Strip! I am not saying that you can't be anything else if you are born in a strip club but that is the first thing you will learn to do.

"If you come up seeing men running around with guns and saying 'Fuck the police and fuck this and that,' that is what you will do."

He revealed that he had been kicked out of school at 16 and had just stayed on the block, which according to him, is where he had been born.

When he was little, he watched and learned a lot from the elders. As he got older, he would sell weed, look for money, pull robberies and do bad things to get through in life.

While your environment is no excuse for committing crime, it is recommended that Governments need to have a long term consistent investment in at-risk communities. To see a reduction in crime, one has to bring about real change. As one person suggested. "Using Greenfield for example - there are people in Greenfield with poor housing structure, poor road facilities and poor infrastructure in terms of lighting and water. These circumstances have never changed in all the years since Independence."

So what do you expect?

One activist posed this question: "Do you expect that the people in an area like Greenfield will automatically reflect a life that is different from the circumstances that they dwell in? The answer is no. If you put a man in a jungle, he will be a beast. If you put him in a castle, he will be a king.

One does not hear about any physical development for the Pine, one does not hear about physical development for the Orleans. You will hear about physical development for Bridgetown or St Lawrence Gap. This is because people believe this is where the economy of the people is, *but more important to the economy of the country is its social stability.*

"So if one builds up the economy in these areas and neglects the social stability in these low-income communities, it is not hard to see that one day, one will spill over into the next – the instability will undermine and negate that economic development is being sought.

"Neglecting the communities and neglecting the families by not doing significant infrastructural, social, economic investments in these communities will cause problems in the long run. If you put people in the ghetto, some people will escape it, but a percentage of that population will take on the characteristics, feel and look of the society that they live in."

One man said "If you go through the Pine, there are a lot of men (and families) living in shanties in 2022. This man living in the shanty will develop a deep resentment towards society when he sees other people reflecting a more advanced form of living, running water and nice big houses.

"Many youths in low-income communities get bullied because others feel they are 'too bright.' Any time you strive to be better in these communities, there is a lot of negative reaction you have to endure." These sentiments were echoed by a businessman in a lower-income urban community who said that he received a lot of negativity when he expanded his business and tried to expand his home.

This feeling has become intrinsic in people's characteristics and behaviour. Resentment breeds jealousy and malice. "It is a serious thing. So that when a man gets a car, others will quickly accuse him of thinking that he is better than anybody else." This is the genesis of the crab in the barrel syndrome.

"When a man is in dire straits, and he feels neglected, he will be angry. And this begets severely antisocial behaviour. Behaviour is ingrained and not entrenched in these communities because it is a learnt behaviour – nothing changes. It is generational – nothing changes. If one grows up and sees change, one is likely to move with the change. If one does not see change however, one will merely continue along the same way. It is important to stress here that not everyone in the community will react similarly.

"Sometimes you need to move people out of the environment they are in. There have been known successes of moving gang members out of the communities, putting them into skills training programmes and getting them into jobs. These individuals never went back into that gang lifestyle. Sometimes, just showing people that you care helps significantly.

"You cannot come into communities with empty promises. You also have to let men know the reality of things as well – there is no magic wand change. For the change to happen, you have to invest in it yourself. So sending a man to skills training is not the beginning or the end of his change – he has to understand he has a commitment to finish the programme and to search for better for himself as well.

"It will not work for everyone. Unfortunately, some of them you have to bury. There are some men who have passed on that you could never get converted. They HAD to die.

"Take warning," says the activist. "If you do not pay attention and invest in low-income communities, the de facto rulers will take over – the underground will rule. Look at Tivoli Gardens and the Dudus Coke situation in Jamaica where neglecting Tivoli resulted in the Presidential Click empire run by Coke. These rulers see opportunities to build an army. If Government does not do what they are supposed to do, then the underground government will do it. They will get commitment by giving a man a pair of shoes and other material things and they will build commitment and build their army that way.

"If Government does not give a man the means to help himself, then the underground like Dudus Coke and others in the region will take over. Barbadians have their neighbours to see what is going on and what can potentially happen and they need to pay attention.

"There were discussions in the past to look at community-by-community and engage in transforming each area but it never materialized. The plan was to build up the infrastructure - fix the roads, remove the graffiti and all the negative images, improve the houses and create social programmes but the plans fell through.

"Sometimes the community influences behaviour, rather than the individual influencing the community."

However, the responsibility is not all on Government. People need to take more responsibility for their behaviours.

CHAPTER TWENTY

Discussion

This book has explored ***gang and street culture*** by investigating this issue within a historical context by way of examining research on gangs; through the interviewing of stakeholders including former police officers, interviews with current and former members of gangs and community activists. This research has unearthed some recurring themes worthy of analysis and discussion.

At the core of the problem of gang and gun violence is the easy availability of firearms and organized crime complicit with the corruption of some public officials and business persons. These realities, coupled with structural issues such as unemployment, poverty, social exclusion, lack of role models and a need to belong make it easier for criminals to engage in deadly violence with perceived impunity.

The main themes emerging from this book are:
- ✓ Lack of role models
- ✓ The gang/group as family
- ✓ Masculinity and crime
- ✓ Alienation/social exclusion
- ✓ Respect
- ✓ Misplaced values
- ✓ Corruption
- ✓ Power and control

We will unpack each of these themes.

Lack of role models

When one analyses the background of most persons who run afoul of the law, it is evident that positive role models are lacking in their lives. Many young men are raised in less-than-optimal environments, where there is no father figure, or in those cases where there *is* a father present, he is not enforcing positive values and displaying indifference towards his role. The role model becomes the boss on the street. The push/pull factor where there is something missing in the home is easily provided on the block.

This book has also revealed that in many situations, parents enable the deviant behaviour of their children. Research has shown that they are the ones who give their children their first ounce of marijuana or in some cases, a gun.

This leads to the other theme:

The gang/group as a family

Most gang research addresses this theme. The gang is seen as a family structure, and indeed many gangs dismiss the fact that they are even gangs. "We are not a gang. We are just a family who looks out for each other," say most of these men. This is a common view emanating from both current and former gang members when asked how they would see themselves. These men live as a brotherhood and it is very evident when one speaks to them. They cook for each other (going back to the days of Kool and the Gang from the 1970's), live as a family, and lift each other up. They reprimand, scold and even fall out with each other, sometimes in a lethal way, but they generally are a brotherhood and fiercely defend each other as a group when it is necessary.

The family also has a hierarchical structure with established roles. There is the boss, who is the leader of the gang/block and his lieutenants who in many cases idolize and protect him. It is a symbiotic relationship between power and the exploitation of weaknesses in vulnerable young men. Many of these men are looking for love - a role model and the need to belong (to anything). It is a costly enterprise – values are eroded and loyalty bought, by material things, which is usually the prized outcome of this relationship.

It has been noted that many men just want to be a part of a grouping. This speaks to the need to belong to something. Many of them crave being in the group because of the notoriety of the group. The group is one which is notorious and one to be feared. Many of the men interviewed admitted that strangers wanted to be part of their group because of whom or what they represented. When they had proven themselves on the streets as a group to be feared and respected, others gravitated toward them.

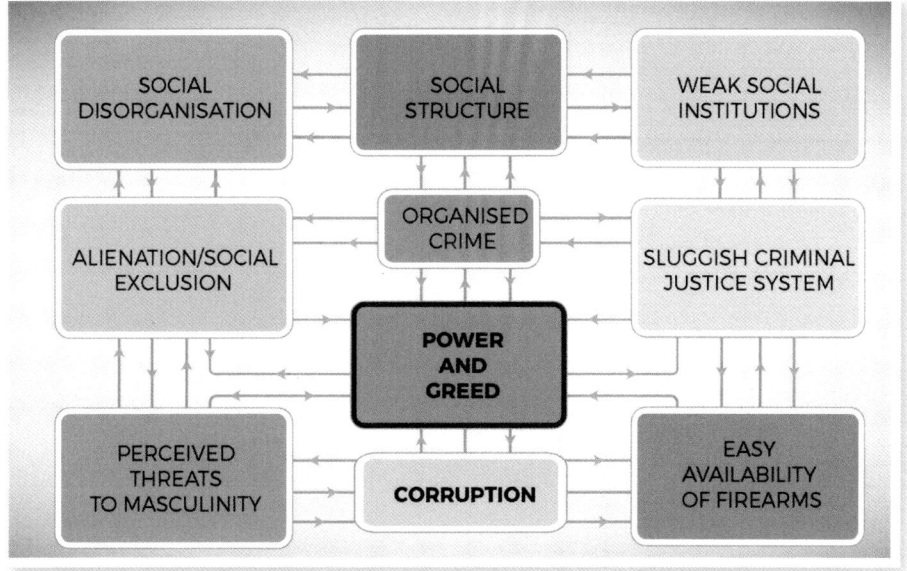

Figure 02: The Main Drivers Of Crime

Power, greed and control:

Power, and its close ally greed, are the drivers of many of the social ills including crime. Power is a force – it lies at the heart of men. It brings respect, fame and fortune. It can also be manipulated to victimize and exploit. It is an overwhelming craving of many - to be powerful and to be relevant.

Whether one operates in the boardroom, in the office, or in the streets; whether one is a CEO or a boss/don on the streets, one is a leader with men/women at one's beck and call. One can dictate orders and delegate to subordinates. This sense of power and control is intoxicating. In many cases, it can be an extremely dangerous weapon to wield.

On the streets, a gun is a symbol of power. Men invest in guns for protection. In a subculture where it is 'Kill or be killed', a gun for many men is seen as a necessity.

Masculinity and crime

When these men feel that their masculinity is threatened or needs to be proven, or they feel 'dissed', the desire to start a war, a fight to prove themselves is compelling. One man on the streets explained that his friend from an urban street crew was dissatisfied that his name was not 'blinging' on the streets, and felt like starting something.

The streets kept him relevant whereas in mainstream society, he is considered a nobody, even a nuisance. It cannot ever be underestimated the power of this desire to prove oneself on the street and garner respect.

An analysis of street murders and shootings reveal that the vast majority of them starts from simple altercations that then mushrooms and explodes into deeper and more serious conflicts.

Many authors have concluded that while there may be some evidence for the early propensity of aggression in boys, the majority of violent behaviour is explained by social factors during adolescence and childhood. In other words, boys are not born violent – they **learn** to be violent. And they mainly learn to be violent by seeing other boys and men use violence, engaging in violent computer games, or by witnessing violence, or by themselves being victims of violence in the home, at school and in their neighbourhood. They see violence as effective means to acquire income, power, respect and attract women. Unexposed to any other ways of resolving conflict, they learn that violence is the *only* swift way to resolve conflict.

In addition, a man is usually socialized into violence as an expected response simply because he *is* a man. We place social roles and behaviours on both men and women from birth and this follows them through their lives. Those who study gender will agree that masculinity is discussed as doing gender, where a man is to be strong, ruthless, show prowess and not to be emotional. To deviate from this is seen as being soft and even effeminate. Unfortunately, many men are socialized in this way, especially by the females that raise them and by wider society.

Young men who cannot get attention for other qualities or achieve identity through other means may find that being a tough guy is better than going unnoticed. Acts that are labelled by teachers and parents as risky or antisocial behaviour may be ways for the individual to prove himself or become part of a group, or simply to be recognised for something, anything which lifts him out of anonymity.

For some young men, becoming a gang member provides a sense of belonging, a source of income, status and being feared/respected. Frustrations over social exclusion are now turned on their heads. Young men in gangs seem to say 'Instead of me fearing you, you will fear me.'

Gang members achieve status through force and brutality, but they _do_ achieve that longed and craved for status.

Alienation/social exclusion

We have dedicated a chapter addressing this phenomenon of social exclusion. It is at the heart of many of the challenges seen in inner city and other communities, where neglect, discrimination and alienation are real issues.

Persons from some communities in Barbados admit that their communities are historically labeled as 'bad' communities and this has affected their social lives, their job prospects and their general well-being. This discrimination is the plight of many from these communities.

With poor job prospects, labelling and discrimination comes neglect. Emerging from this neglect springs the underground government which facilitates/enables the exploitation of community members.

Respect

Respect is the cornerstone of street culture. Many conflicts are started because of a perceived lack of respect. For many of these men, it is all they desire – traditional society has already failed them, written them off, labelled them as failures and to a large extent, nonentities - but the streets offer that space where they can successfully craft and establish/demand respect for themselves.

Respect is usually achieved by being ruthless, gaining street creds, being feared and having access to and being intimate with many women. On the streets, these characteristics are sought after. To be anything less makes you lose credibility on the streets.

Misplaced values

What has been interesting to observe is that many so-called bad boys and gangsters have their own moral compass. It is a somewhat contradictory value system where there are certain behaviours that are looked down on. Stealing from the poor and underprivileged is scorned. While some of these men have engaged in heinous crimes, including shootings, extortion, choppings and other activities, they feel strongly about attributes such as good manners and respect for your elders. They see a thief or a burglar as the worst form of criminal and are quick to say that while they have committed robberies, snatched men's chains or transported cocaine, at least they "never broke into anyone's house". One man said "True gangsters do not break houses or snatch bags".

Corruption

One thing that is incontrovertible is that corruption breeds criminal activity. Corruption is at the core of organized crime in most communities. Persons from all strata of society, including the higher echelons - business persons and government officials - are alleged to be involved in drug and gun racketeering. The tentacles stretch far, wide and deep. Until these tentacles are cut off at the source, we are indeed fighting a losing battle against crime and gang activity.

Corruption must be weeded out in order to ensure that processes can work effectively. One must look at the books of business people and their investments. According to one resident, "If the top does nothing, it will get worse."

In 2019, The Government of Barbados introduced a new bill in Parliament called the **Proceeds and Instrumentalities of Crime Bill 2019-7.** This bill essentially targets persons who benefit from the proceeds of crime and come into assets through unlawful means, with the intention of depriving them of these ill gotten assets. This legislation makes it clear that persons who have benefited from crime as far back as 20 years prior to the enactment of the legislation will also be targeted. One of the most important aspects of the bill is the Unexplained Wealth Orders where police can charge a person under this act if there are grounds to believe that a person has accumulated wealth illegitimately. There are forfeiture orders where there is provision for seizure of cash and other assets.

We need to take the profit out of crime. Once crime is lucrative, it will always be prevalent. The Act mentioned above, once enforced is a step in the right direction of reduction of organised crime and corruption.

CHAPTER TWENTY ONE

Solutions

We have discussed the problems and causes of gun and street violence. The solutions are more multifaceted and must be engaged in at the micro and macro level.

Structural changes

"It is important to invest in socially disadvantaged communities," one stakeholder has recommended. "Invest more in **quality** education, not just education. Invest in the infrastructure of communities, the way they look." This goes a long way in positively changing the psychological and social makeup of a community.

In Trinidad, prisoners were taken into poor communities to do a very simple thing: paint all the sidewalks white. That simple thing made a difference. People in these communities started to feel good about themselves, believing that they were finally getting attention. Painting the sidewalks uplifted the aesthetics of the physical environment, and by extension their psychosocial responses. People's behaviours change when these things take place. People were then encouraged to create gardens and beautify their communities. These are, admittedly, simple things, but they can ignite much grander improvements which have the capacity to uplift the entire community.

Unfortunately, as often happens, this project in Trinidad was not sustained.

Changing behaviour is not just about what people tell you to do – it is about what you see. Reflections – it is like a mirror image. If a person keeps seeing around themselves and by extension, themselves as ghetto, they will behave "ghetto". According to the stakeholder "ghetto" symbolizes poverty and graffiti walls, garbage spilled on the streets and unkempt neighbourhoods". All these are the things we have to change!

Unemployment and poverty are inextricably linked to crime as well. This is one of the root causes of crime. The recent ash programme gave many unemployed persons an opportunity to be part of the labour force. It is hoped that the development of skills will go a long way in making these persons employable in the future.

We also have to enforce our laws, and jail people who want to break the law with impunity. "We have to understand that this world has bad people," one individual interviewed stressed. "No matter what you do, some people are bad and some have psychological issues that are not going to change. A lot of people have unresolved issues and suffer from trauma."

Trauma is a constant reality in many persons who offend or are at risk of offending. Unfortunately, many persons who suffer from some form of trauma are not usually treated for this trauma. There is a need for early interventions through more psychosocial programmes for at-risk and vulnerable persons to treat to their traumatic life experiences as these have the potential to negatively shape their behaviour and place them more at risk to enter the criminal justice system.

"There are not enough jobs out there for everyone, so you need the marijuana trade," opined a resident. "You must create employment for poor people." To him, the trade was a poor, black man's response which was helping communities. Effectively, this is about survival and the view is that without the drug trade, many persons within inner city communities will simply resort to other crimes in order to survive. Unfortunately, it is not as simple as that. The drug trade has caused many wars and led to the death of many young men due to the nature of the business.

One community activist believes that the most viable solution is mediation - sitting down, talking, creating more positive activities, and going to the heart and not the peripheral. "Go to the leaders to solve the war. The model of bringing together the warring leaders worked in the Pine, and could work with other warring groups, bringing together the leaders who are leading the gangs," the activist forcefully declared. This will have a trickle-down effect when the young men who see these men as their role models, and who are warring with each other based on gang affiliation, will come together when they see that their leaders have done the same.

"The model of bringing warring groups can be replicated, working with the community arm of the Police Service," he maintained.

There is also the recommendation that in order to address the issues in the community, a **Barbadian** approach is needed; arts and sports are two major planks in resolving the problem.

There was also the suggestion of zoning the island. "Put the country into zones, look at 34 housing areas or more that exist in Barbados and put physical police outposts. They can look at the community centres where the community officers are based. Change the name from 'Community Centres' to 'Resource Centres' which reflects a multi-sectoral, multi-dimensional approach to crime solving in Barbados."

Inter-community issues change over time. They can be prevented with the right introductory measures in the community. The best way to stop gun violence is to have serious community intervention.

We must also create safe and positive spaces for our young people. These spaces must be sustainable. These spaces must be kept safe from violence, from conflict, from domestic issues. They should also nurture a learning, caring environment where life skills and other skills are taught.

Another recommendation is that at all ports of entry, police, soldiers and customs officers, should create a task force where they work together as a team to patrol and conduct searches.

Treating violence as a public health concern

Discussion on treating violence as a public health issue has been extensively discussed. It is imperative that governments in the region treat the issue of crime as such, using the models offered by agencies and criminologists to curb the uptake in violence in the region. The Centres for Disease Control and Prevention outlines a four-step process to tackle violence which, according to them is scientific and can be applied not only to violence but any other health problem affecting a society.

- Phase 1: Defining and Monitoring the Problem
- Phase 2: Identifying Risk and Protective Factors that are correlated to crime
- Phase 3: Developing Prevention Strategies
- Phase 4: Widespread Adoption

We can also look to our neighbours for lessons learnt. Community efforts such as the Peace Management Initiative and Dispute Resolution Foundation in Jamaica have reaped rewards. These initiatives work with warring factions in communities to mediate and establish ceasefires and community codes of conduct. They also teach conflict resolution skills in the communities. Again, these initiatives need to be long-term and sustainable.

More programmes need to offered to boys on the block who wish to leave the life of the streets and lead more productive lives through the teaching of skills including soft skills and leadership skills for future positive employment opportunities.

There is also the option of the introduction of sporting programmes with anti-violence messages as well as teaching conflict resolution as a part of these sporting programmes.

Work with young men to remove the association of masculinity with violence

Many men who are involved in the street culture associate guns and aggression with strength and manhood. This occurs when these young persons do not have the requisite skill set to effectively display their masculinity in any other way than resorting to violence. The community also plays a major role in assisting these young men in finding more appropriate ways to deal with conflict.

The process of preparing for a life of violence begins early. Young children mimic the colours, dress code and behaviours of elders and are indoctrinated into a culture of violence and weapons use, which they see as normal. As a result, family values break down and the community is fractured.

Hence, the community is also an appropriate setting for influencing youth positively and addressing violence. This means that a key characteristic of successful community-based anti-violence strategies is the identification by the community of violence as a problem, which then can lead to interventions specific to its local context.

This is critical as communities have distinct problems and unique demographic, cultural and other characteristics that must be appreciated.

Lastly, and most importantly, many of our young people, particularly young men, need to be properly mentored. Some of them lack guidance, proper role models, have no future goals and are merely meandering their way through life. They see the blocks as safe spaces – to get away from the stresses of family life. While this may be the case in some situations, (as not all blocks are bad spaces), there are some spaces which are not safe. As was evidenced in this book, many young boys look to the gang leader as their mentor, and one to be emulated. There is a need for early intervention with vulnerable and at-risk persons from birth to teenage years, where targeted mentoring and other social programmes should be implemented to deter these populations from a life of crime.

It is important to invest in meaningful Poverty Alleviation Programmes as well as direct investment in our young people in the form of early prevention programmes. It is cheaper to invest in them through prevention rather than spend it after they have become perpetrators in the criminal justice system.

ADDENDUM

Is History Repeating Itself?

"A small body of determined spirits fired by an unquenchable faith in their mission can alter the course of history." – Mohandas Gandhi.

Shortly after completing this book, on Friday, February 24, 2023, the news broke in Barbados that two warring 'groups', the 64 Government, also known as the Red Sea and the Chop City Cartel, both from the urban communities of Deacons and Chapman Lane, respectively, had brokered a truce and decided to stop the existing war.

The meeting, spearheaded by a former elder of the streets, Winston "Iston Bull" Branch, was convened in Chapman Lane, St Michael where according to him, over 200 men from the opposing groups came together and decided to give way to peace and discontinue a war which has been ongoing for several years.

This story made national headlines and has been the hot topic of discussion on social media and even call in programmes for a number of days. Those who have been discussing it are divided in their response. Many see it as a positive step forward to reducing gun violence on the streets. Many lives have been lost over this long war. Many have also been incarcerated. The identification with/allegiance to either gang has spread into schools and the prisons, where the latter has recently had to establish an Anti-Gang Unit to quell the several disturbances within the prison walls, resulting from gang activity associated with either these groups or other groupings.

Peace initiatives are not new and are often recommended as **one** of the solutions to gun violence. In fact, in the chapter presenting Solutions, I have recommended this as one approach to solving the problem of gang and group wars.

These truces also are not new in Barbados. In Chapter 2 on The Pine, a peace treaty was agreed to and the two main gangs/groups came together and established a truce. (Please see Chapter 2 The Pine and Chapter 8 Kool and the Gang). It seemed to have worked, as the groups never had any residual conflict.

That said, it is important to interrogate whether this will work in these circumstances either in the short, medium or long term. The challenges are highlighted below:

As opposed to the Pine war, which was concentrated within that one community, and the war between Kool and the Gang and Sly and the Family Stone which was between neighbouring groups, the war between the 64s and Choppers is not a confined war. There are persons who identify with these groups all over the island.

As a result, many of these persons are not known to the leaders of these groups, and who, some may argue, cannot be 'controlled'. There are persons who just want to be associated, and are not interested in peace. These factors create a significant problem as there can emerge a situation of a lone wolf or even a loose cannon who is trigger-happy, has a problem with anger, or has to settle a score. One community activist recalls the war in the Pine where there was one person who was vehemently against peace and continued to war with others. He was subsequently gunned down.

The years 2007 and 2023 have more than just time between them. Society has evolved. The young men in 2023 have different characteristics to the young men in 2007. As discussed throughout this book, today's men are not interested in listening to the elders of *'The Streets'*, and have basically chosen to ignore them. They are easy to anger, violent and have an insatiable need to prove themselves on the streets. This mindset in itself is a grave challenge.

Most importantly, while a truce has been established, the basic structure and organization of gang activity, vis-a-vis organized crime still exists. There has been no dismantling of the structure, the organization and the ethos of the groupings that caused the violence in the first place. Perhaps, this will be stage two, because merely announcing that there is a truce will **NOT** resolve the problem of gun violence or even wars between groups on the streets.

A phased approach where men in particular, relinquish their weapons to authorities, are assisted with alternatives to gang violence and given opportunities for successful employment, with supporting social and hard skills, is integral to the ultimate success of the accomplishment of this initiative.